THE ARTHRITIS
HELPBOOK

THE ARTHRITIS HELPBOOK

A Tested Self-Management Program
for Coping with Your Arthritis

Revised Edition

Kate Lorig, R.N., Dr.P.H.
Director, Patient Education Research
Stanford Arthritis Center

James F. Fries, M.D.
Associate Professor of Medicine
Stanford University School of Medicine

Contributing Authors

Maureen R. Gecht, O.T.R./L Occupational Therapist
Genevieve E.S. Gines, M.P.H. Specializing in
    International Health
Lynn A. Kaplan, O.T.R./L Occupational Therapist
Dennis M. Keane, M.P.H. Health Educator
BarbaraTerry Kurtz, M.S.W., M.P.H. Social Worker
Doris Meyer, O.T.R. Occupational Therapist
Ingrid Sausjord Moore, R.D., M.P.H. Nutritionist
Sharona Silverman, M.P.H. Health Educator
Deborah Stinchfield, R.P.T. Physical Therapist

ADDISON-WESLEY PUBLISHING COMPANY, INC.
Reading, Massachusetts • Menlo Park, California
New York • Don Mills, Ontario • Wokingham, England
Amsterdam • Bonn • Sydney • Singapore • Tokyo
Madrid • San Juan

Library of Congress Cataloging-in-Publication Data

Lorig, Kate.
  The arthritis helpbook.

  Bibliography: p.
  1. Arthritis — Treatment.   2. Exercise therapy.
3. Self-care, Health.   I. Fries, James F.
II. Title.
RC933.L628   1986   616.7′22   86-13985
ISBN 0-201-05468-X

Many of the designations used by manufacturers and sellers to distinguish their products are claimed as trademarks. Where those designations appear in this book, and Addison-Wesley was aware of a trademark claim, the designations have been printed in initial caps or all caps (i.e. Tylenol).

Graphics by Sharon Leibolt Hathaway
Cover design by Steve Snider
Set in 10-point Melior by Compset, Inc., Beverly, MA

EFGHIJ-DO-898

Fifth Printing, October 1988

To our more than 800 leaders
and to over 20,000
Arthritis Self-Help class participants

Acknowledgments

We would like especially to thank the Stanford Arthritis Center folks: Pat Spitz, Gene Fauro Pratt, Dee Simpson, Beth Kant, Audrey Schomer, R. Guy Kraines, Jim Standish, Alison Harlow, Cathy Williams, Dr. Dennis McShane, Dr. Jeffrey Brown, Dr. Cody Wasner, Dr. Paul Feigenbaum, Dr. Halsted Holman, Dr. Andrei Calin, Dr. Melvin Britton, Dr. Tom Okarma, Dr. William Lages, Dr. David Schurman, Patricia Schweikert, Pam Shelby, Wade Gray, and Rebecca Pronchick. The Midpeninsula Health Service people: Dr. Joseph Hopkins, Judy Staples, Debbie Ridley, Joan Willingham, Jeanne Ewy, Dori Smith, Mary Ann Goodrich, Luann Ciccone, Virginia de Lemos, Sally Semans, and Sarah Reese. The University of California at Berkeley Health Education Faculty: Dr. Robert Miller, Dr. Andrew Fisher, Dr. William Griffiths, Dr. Meredith Minkler, Dr. Carol D'Onofrio, and Dr. John Ratcliffe. Significant others: Dr. Robert Swezey, John Staples, Donna Holsten, Carol Rice, Jane Dito, Marie Cascio, Bea Mandel, Dr. Lawrence Green, Dr. Sarah Archer, Janice Pigg, Gary Katz, Chuck Hamilton, Lila Stricker, Judi Sobieski, Dr. Floyd Pennington, Dr. Stan Shoor, Dr. Peter Wood, Melinda Seeger, Dr. Larry Bradley, Michele Boutaugh, Roseanne Glick, Dr. Ann O'Leary, and Gail Schreiber. Bonnie Obrig and Sharon Joseph performed yeoman service in manuscript preparation as did Genoa Shepley in editing. To all these fine people our deepest appreciation.

Contents

Preface

Before we start we would like to say a little about how this book came to be written and what we have learned in the process.

In 1979 the Stanford Arthritis Center began giving lessons to persons with arthritis. (From the very beginning our class members told us that they did not want to be called "patients.") The classes were taught by 40 people from our community who have arthritis or who are interested in arthritis. With a few exceptions, the teachers were not health professionals. The Arthritis Center staff worked with the teachers, and the lay teachers led the classes.

Our arthritis education classes use the same principles that we have presented earlier in *Take Care of Yourself, Taking Care of Your Child,* and *Arthritis: A Comprehensive Guide,* and they have benefited greatly from the many thousands of encouraging letters and helpful suggestions we have received. In these classes we are not concerned solely with improving knowledge. We also seek to help persons with arthritis change their activities and abilities, decrease their pain, and most importantly, develop more confidence in themselves as caretakers for their bodies.

In our classes we emphasize three concepts:

1. Each person with arthritis is different. There is no one treatment that is right for everyone.

2. There are a number of things people can do to feel better. These things will not cure most kinds of arthritis, but they will help to relieve pain, maintain or increase mobility, and prevent deformity.

3. With knowledge, each individual is the best judge of which self-management techniques are best for him or her.

Therefore, this book was developed to give details about a variety of self-management treatments. We felt that it was not enough just to know that you should exercise. Instead, you must know about particular exercises, types of exercise, when to exercise, and how much to exercise. You need to understand the relationship between exercise and pain. The same considerations hold for what you need to know about relaxation, nutrition, problem solving, and all other self-management techniques. In *Arthritis: A Comprehensive Guide* we provided all the factual knowledge about arthritis. In this companion volume we try to help you use the information. This is a how-to-do-it book that has been developed with the help of many people very much like you.

When our class members first used this book they liked it but were quick to point out its faults: a neck exercise that caused too much pain, a nutrition section that was unclear, omission of a section on sleep disturbances, and so forth. Taking these suggestions we have added, revised, clarified, re-used, re-revised in a continuing cycle that has resulted in this present edition.

While only eleven names appear on the title page as authors and contributors, this book was really written and guided by you, people with arthritis. As of late 1986, more than 20,000 people have attended these classes and used this book. From all of them we have gained insights that we hope will be helpful to you.

All these people helped us in other ways, too. We have been carefully studying the effect of our classes on the way that people get along with their arthritis, and our class members have served as the subjects for these studies. In effect we "drew straws" to see which of the subjects on the waiting list would attend the next set of classes and which would have to wait four months. Then we compared how the people who went to the classes did with how the people on the waiting list did. Data from long questionnaries went into the computer, and after elaborate analyses we found what we had suspected all along.

People who become good arthritis self-managers have less pain and are more active than those people who feel there is nothing they can do for themselves. These are the first controlled studies that have ever been done relating education programs in arthritis to outcomes, and they are very encouraging. The bottom line is that arthritis self-managers feel better! We would like to help you become an arthritis self-manager.

Now a few words of caution. First, you did not get stiff, painful joints overnight. Therefore, relief will not come quickly. Self-management is in no way a quick cure; it is a way of life to be practiced every day for the rest of your life. However, it is never too late to start. Our oldest self-manager was 96 when she first came to class.

Second, not everything works for everyone. Experiment, but give each activity two weeks to a month for first results. Don't give up too soon. If one thing does not work for you, try another.

Finally, this book is not meant to replace medical care. Rather, it is a supplement to that care. Most doctors do not have or do not take the time to explain exercises or pain-management techniques in enough detail to help you very much. Therefore, we are hopeful that this book will assist both you and your physician. All of the advice and activities that we describe have been reviewed by many, many doctors, physical therapists, occupational therapists, nutritionists, and nurses, including the entire staff of the Stanford Arthritis Center. They represent a sound program essentially the same as that recommended by most health authorities today. If you have particular questions please talk them over with your doctor.

We would like you to feel that you are part of our cast of thousands. If you have comments or suggestions please send them to us by writing:

Stanford Arthritis Center
HRP Building, Room 6
Stanford, California 94305

Your suggestions will be reviewed and considered for our next edition. To all of you who helped in the past and who we couldn't name, many thanks, and to those of you who are just joining, a hearty welcome.

Stanford, California   K. L.

August 1986   J. F. F.

THE ARTHRITIS
HELPBOOK

1

Arthritis
What Is It?

Arthritis. The very word evokes a specter of fear and pain. People think of getting old, being unable to get around, and of becoming more dependent upon others. More so than with any other disease, the term "arthritis" carries with it a sense of hopelessness and futility. But the very opposite should be true. All arthritis can be helped.

In order to understand how to work with your arthritis, it is necessary to know a little about it. In fact, arthritis is not just a single disease. There are over 100 kinds of arthritis, all of which have something to do with one or more joints in the body. Even the word *arthritis* is misleading. The *arth* part comes from the Greek word meaning "joint," while *itis* means "inflammation or infection." Thus the word *arthritis* means "inflammation of the joint." The problem is that in many kinds of arthritis, the joint is not inflamed. A better description might be "problems with the joint."

The next step is to understand what a joint looks like and what the various parts do.

WHERE ARTHRITIS ATTACKS

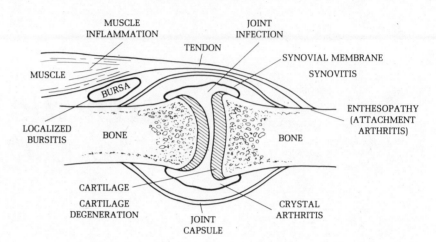

A joint is a meeting of two bones for the purpose of allowing movement. It has the following six parts.

1. **Cartilage.** The end of each bone is covered with cartilage, a tough material that cushions and protects the ends of the bone. To get some idea of what cartilage is like, feel the middle of your nose or your ears. These are also made of cartilage. Cartilage in meat is "gristle."

2. **Synovial membrane (synovial sac).** Around each joint is the synovial sac, which protects the joint and also secretes the synovial fluid, which oils the joint. In fact, this fluid has many times the lubricating power of oil.

3. **Bursa.** A bursa is a small sac that is not part of the joint but is near the joint. It contains a fluid that lubricates the movement of muscles: muscle across muscle and muscle across bones. In some ways it is similar to the synovial sac.

4. **Muscle.** The muscles are elastic tissues that, by becoming shorter and longer, move the bones and thus move you.

5. **Tendon.** The tendons are fibrous cords that attach the muscles to the bones. You can feel them on the back of your hand or in the back of your knee.

6. **Ligament.** The ligaments are much shorter fibrous cords that attach bone to bone and make up the joint capsules.

When someone says, "I have arthritis," it means that something is wrong with one or more of these parts. For example, when the synovial membrane becomes inflamed, this is true arthritis. That is, the joint is inflamed. However, if the muscle becomes stretched from overexercise or is injured, this is not arthritis. The joint itself is not affected.

In each major kind of arthritis, a different joint tissue is involved. In *rheumatoid arthritis*, the problem is chiefly "synovitis," that is, an inflammation of the synovial membrane. This inflammation must be reduced with medication in addition to your self-management program. In *ankylosing spondylitis*, the problem is an "enthesopathy," an inflammation where the ligaments attach to the bone. This inflammation also needs to be suppressed by medication, and the affected joints need to be regularly and vigorously stretched. In *osteoarthritis*, the problem is a breakdown of the joint cartilage, but it is helped by exercise and proper use of your joints. In *gout*, the problem is crystals which form in the joint space and cause inflammation and pain. Each kind of arthritis is different, and different treatment is needed.

While there are over 100 types of arthritis, we discuss in detail only the major types. If you are interested in knowing more about other types of arthritis, read *Arthritis: A Comprehensive Guide*, by Dr. James F. Fries (Reading, Mass.: Addison-Wesley, 1986).

2

Rheumatoid Arthritis
Inflamed Joints

Rheumatoid arthritis (RA) is more than just arthritis. Indeed, many doctors call it "rheumatoid disease" to emphasize its widespread nature. The name is trying awkwardly to say the same thing; the term *rheum* refers to the stiffness, body aching, and fatigue that often accompany rheumatoid arthritis. Persons with RA often describe feeling much like they have a virus, with fatigue and aching in the muscles, except that, unlike a usual viral illness, the condition may persist for months or even years.

About one-half of one percent of our population has rheumatoid arthritis, some one million individuals in the United States. Most of these people (about three-quarters) are women. The condition usually appears in middle life, in the forties or fifties, although it can begin at any age. Rheumatoid arthritis in children is quite different. Rheumatoid arthritis has been medically identified for about 200 years, although bone changes in the skeletons of some Mexican Indian groups suggest that the disease may have been around for thousands of years.

Since RA is so common, and because it can sometimes be severe, it is a major national health problem. It can result in difficulties with employment, problems with daily activities, and can put a severe stress on family relationships. In its most severe forms, and without good treatment, it can result in deformities of the joints. Fortunately, most people with RA do well and lead normal lives. Fear of rheumatoid arthritis, sometimes greatly exaggerated, can be as harmful as the disease itself.

In RA, the synovial membrane lining in the joint becomes inflamed. We don't have a good explanation as to why this inflammation starts, but the cells in the membrane divide and grow, and inflammatory cells come into the joint. Because of the bulk of these inflammatory cells, the joint becomes swollen, and feels puffy or boggy to the touch. The increased blood flow that is a feature of the inflammation makes the joint warm. The cells release chemicals (called *enzymes*) into the joint space and the enzymes cause further irritation and pain. If the process continues for years, the enzymes may gradually digest the cartilage and bone of the joint, actually eating away parts of the bone.

This then is rheumatoid arthritis, a process in which inflammation of the joint membrane, over many years, can cause damage to the joint itself.

FEATURES

Swelling and pain in one or more joints, lasting at least six weeks, are required for a diagnosis of rheumatoid arthritis. Usually, both sides of the body are affected similarly, and the arthritis is said to be "symmetrical." Often there are slight differences between the two sides, usually the right side being slightly worse in right-handed people and vice versa. Occasionally the condition skips about in an erratic fashion. The wrists and knuckles are almost always involved. The knees and the joints of the ball of the foot are often involved as well, and any joint can be affected. Of the knuckles, those at the base of the fingers are most frequently painful, while the joints at the ends of the fingers are often normal.

Lumps, usually between the size of a pea and a mothball, may form beneath the skin. These *rheumatoid nodules* are most commonly located near the elbow at the place where you rest your arms on the table, but they can pop up anywhere. Each represents an inflammation of a small blood vessel. They come and go during the course of the illness and usually are not a big problem. They do tend to occur in people with the most severe kinds of RA. Rarely, they become sore or infected, particularly if they are located around the ankle. Even more rarely, they form in the lungs or elsewhere in the body.

Laboratory tests sometimes can help a doctor recognize rheumatoid arthritis. The *rheumatoid factor* or *latex fixation* is the most commonly used blood test. Although this test may be negative in the first several months, it is eventually positive in about 80 percent of persons with RA. The rheumatoid factor is actually an antibody to certain body proteins and can sometimes be found in individuals with other diseases. Some doctors think that it is a way the body fights the disease, others think that it may play a role in causing the joint damage.

The *sed rate* is another frequently used blood test. This test is called in full an *erythrocyte sedimentation rate* and the name sometimes is abbreviated ESR. It doesn't help in diagnosis, but it does help tell the severity of the disease. A high sed rate (over 30 or so) suggests that the disease is quite active. The joint fluid is sometimes examined in rheumatoid arthritis in order to look at the inflammatory cells or to make sure that the joint is not infected with bacteria.

X-rays are not very helpful in the initial diagnosis of rheumatoid arthritis. It is unusual for changes to be seen in the bones or cartilage in the first few months of the disease, even when it is most severe. X-rays can help the doctor determine if damage to the bones or cartilage has occurred as the disease progresses. Some doctors like to get baseline X-rays to compare with later X-rays; we prefer to minimize the total number of X-rays.

Most people with RA notice problems in parts of their bodies other than the joints themselves. Usually, these are general problems such as muscle aches, fatigue, muscle stiffness (particularly in the morning), and even a low fever. Morning stiffness is often considered a hallmark of RA and is sometimes termed the *gel phenomenon*. After a rest period or even after just sitting motionless for a few minutes, the whole body feels stiff and is difficult to move. After a period of loosening up, motion becomes easier and less painful. People often have problems with fluid accumulation, particularly around the ankles. Occasionally, the rheumatoid disease may attack other body tissues, including the whites of the eyes, the nerves, the small arteries, and the lungs. Anemia (low red blood cell count) is quite common, although it is seldom severe enough to need any treatment. Some patients will develop *Sjögren's disease*, or sicca syndrome, in which the tear fluids and the saliva dry up, causing dry eyes and dry mouth. This happens because the lacrimal (tear) glands and the salivary glands become involved in the rheumatoid process.

There can be unusual features due to the inflammation of the joint membrane. A *Baker's cyst* can form behind the knees and may feel like a tumor. It is just the synovial sac full of fluid, but it can extend down into the back of the calf and may cause pain. Or, the fluid in the joint can become infected and require immediate treatment. Suspect this if a single joint, usually a knee, becomes suddenly and severely worse.

Rheumatoid arthritis is one of the most complicated and mysterious diseases known. It is a challenge to patient and physician alike. Fortunately, the course of RA can be dramatically changed in most individuals. More so than with any other form of arthritis, if you have RA you need to develop an effective partnership with your doctor, as discussed in Chapter 15.

PROGNOSIS (THE FUTURE OF THE DISEASE)

Rheumatoid arthritis is the condition that most people think of when they hear the word *arthritis*. An image that comes to mind is of a person in a wheelchair, with swollen knees and twisted hands. True, most such people have rheumatoid arthritis. On balance, rheumatoid arthritis is the most destructive kind of arthritis known. Erosion of the bone itself, rupture of tendons, and slippage of the joints can result in crippling. But most people with rheumatoid arthritis do very, very much better than this. In fact, only one in six persons with RA develops any crippling or deformities at all. And it is probable that these could have been prevented by good, early treatment.

The course of persons with RA usually falls into one of three patterns. The first, and best, is that of a brief illness lasting at most a few months and leaving no disability; this course is sometimes called *monocyclic*. The second involves a series of episodes of illness, separated by periods of being entirely well. This is sometimes termed *polycyclic* and usually does not result in very much physical impairment. The third, termed *chronic*, is a more constant disease lasting a number of years, sometimes for life. Probably the majority of persons with rheumatoid arthritis have this chronic form, but even here, serious crippling is unusual. At first it is hard to be sure which pattern the disease will follow, but a chronic course is suggested by the presence of the rheumatoid factor in a blood test and is strongly suggested if the condition has continued to progress for an entire year.

Often it is hard for persons with RA and their relatives to appreciate that even the worst forms of rheumatoid arthritis tend to get better with time. The arthritis usually becomes less aggressive. The inflammation (synovitis) is less active and the fatigue and stiffness decrease. New joints are less likely to become involved after several years of disease. But even though the disease is less violent, any destruction of bones and ligaments that occurred in earlier years will persist. Thus deformities usually will not improve, even though no new damage is occurring. Hence, it is important to treat the disease correctly in the early years so that the joints will work well after the disease activity subsides.

TREATMENT

Treatment programs for rheumatoid arthritis are often complicated and can be very confusing. In this section we give the broad outlines for sound management. But the combination of measures best for you needs to be worked out with your doctor. It has been said that the person who has himself for a doctor has a fool for a patient. In many areas of medicine, and for some kinds of arthritis, this is not true — you can do just as well looking out for yourself. But with rheumatoid arthritis you do need a doctor. Indeed, if your rheumatoid arthritis is at all severe, you may want to be seen, at least occasionally, but a specialist in arthritis, a *rheumatologist*.

First, some common sense. Your rheumatoid arthritis may be with you, on and off, for months or years. The best treatments are those that will help you maintain a life that is as nearly normal as possible. Often the worst treatments are those that offer immediate relief. They may allow joint damage to progress or may cause delayed side effects that ultimately make you feel worse. So, you must develop some patience with the disease and with its management. You have to adjust your thinking to operate in the same slow time scale that the disease uses. You and your doctor will want to be anticipating problems before they occur so that they may be avoided. The adjustment to a long-term illness, with the necessity to plan treatment programs that may take months to get results, is a difficult psychological task. It is easy to understand in principle but hard to put into daily action. This adjustment will be one of your hardest jobs in battling your arthritis.

Synovitis is the underlying problem. The inflammation of the joint membrane releases enzymes that very slowly damage the joint structures. Good treatment reduces this inflammation and stops the damage. Painkillers can increase comfort but do not decrease the arthritis. In fact, pain per se helps to protect the joints by discouraging too much use. So, in RA it is important to treat pain by treating the inflammation that causes the pain. By and large, pain relievers such as codeine, Percodan, Darvon, or Demerol must be avoided. (To learn more, read Chapter 14.)

The proper balance between rest and exercise is hard to understand. Rest reduces the inflammation, and this is good. But rest also lets joints get stiff and muscles get weak. With too much rest, tendons become less strong and bones get softer. Obviously, this is bad. So, moderation is the basic principle. It may help you to know that your body usually gives you the right signals about what to do and what not to do. If it hurts too much, don't do it. If you don't seem to have much problem with an activity, go ahead. As a general rule, if you continue to have exercise-caused pain for more than two hours after exercising, you have done too much.

A particularly painful joint may require a splint to help it rest. Still, you will want to exercise the joint by stretching it gently in different directions to keep it from getting stiff. You will not want to use a splint for too long, or you may want to use it just at night. As the joint gets better you will want to begin using the joint, gently at first but slowly progressing to more and more activity. In general, favor activities that build good muscle tone, not those that build great muscle strength. Walking and swimming are better than furniture moving and weight lifting, since tasks requiring a lot of strength put a lot of stress across the joint. And regular exercises done daily are better than occasional sprees of activity that unduly stress joints not ready for so much exertion.

Common sense and a regular, long-term program are the keys to success. Should you take a nap after lunch? Yes, if you're tired. Should you undertake some particular outing? Go on a trip? You know your regular daily activity level. Common sense will answer most such questions. Full normal activity should be approached gradually with a long-term conditioning program that includes rest when needed and gradual increases in activity during nonresting periods.

Physical therapists and occupational therapists can often help with specific advice and helpful hints. The best therapists will help you develop your own program for home exercise and will teach you the exercises and activities that will help your joints. However, don't expect the therapist to do your program for you. Your rest and exercise program cannot consist solely of formal sessions at a rehabilitation facility. You must take the responsibility to build the habits that will, on a daily basis, protect and strengthen your joints. It is important to start exercise and proper use of your joints before you have problems. These are good preventive measures.

Medications are required by most persons with rheumatoid arthritis and often must be continued for months or years. By and large, the most powerful drugs have the worst side effects. So, good physicians will begin with the simplest and the safest drugs and will use more hazardous drugs only if the simpler measures are not sufficient. Most people will not require the more powerful drugs.

Aspirin and the newer "nonsteroidal" drugs are useful when used correctly. Every person with arthritis should know all about aspirin. Aspirin is a strong anti-inflammatory drug with an acceptable level of side effects. Drugs roughly similar to aspirin are called *nonsteroidal anti-inflammatory drugs* and are very frequently used. Examples of such drugs are Motrin, Nalfon, Tolectin, Naprosyn, and Indocin. (For more information, see Chapter 14.)

Antimalarial drugs such as chloroquine or Plaquenil are sometimes used next, if the anti-inflammatory agents have not been enough. Gold is often helpful if the previous drugs have not been sufficient and sometimes result in complete disappearance of the arthritis. Penicillamine can also result in dramatic improvement. Azulfidine is a sulfa drug that is now finding new uses in arthritis treatment.

Corticosteroids, most frequently prednisone, are strong hormones with dangerous long-term side effects. Their use is controversial in rheumatoid arthritis; some physicians feel that they should almost never be used, and others use them, but only in very small doses. Immunosuppressant drugs, such as Cytoxan, methotrexate, Imuran, or chlorambucil, are powerful, and potentially hazardous; some physicians still think that these drugs are too dangerous to use in rheumatoid arthritis. Steroids and immunosuppressants are sometimes needed for severe complications such as nerve damage or eye damage.

Surgery sometimes can restore the function of a damaged joint. Hip replacement, knee replacement, and synovectomy (removal of the joint membrane) are the most common operations.

3

Osteoarthritis

Osteoarthritis (osteoarthrosis, OA, degenerative joint disease, DJD) is the kind of arthritis that everybody gets. It is a practically universal problem, increasing with age, and one that, because of its relationship to the aging process, is not as responsive to medical treatment as we might like. However, there are many things you can do for yourself to alleviate this disease. Fortunately, osteoarthritis usually is a relatively mild condition. Osteoarthritis is a much less severe form of arthritis than rheumatoid arthritis. In other words, the changes in the skeleton that occur with age are inevitable, but they cause symptoms in a minority of people and severe symptoms in very few.

Osteoarthritis used to be thought of as the inevitable result of "wear and tear." In fact, most activities with a lot of "wear" don't seem to cause much "tear," and authorities now recognize the need for exercise to strengthen the joints, both before and after signs of arthritis have developed.

The tissue involved in osteoarthritis is the cartilage. This is the gristle material that faces the ends of the bones and forms the surface of the joint on both sides. Gristle is tough, somewhat elastic, and very durable. The cartilage or gristle does not have a blood supply, so it gets its oxygen and nutrition from the surrounding joint fluid. In this it is aided by being elastic and by being able to absorb fluid. When we use a joint, the pressure squeezes fluid and waste products out of the cartilage, and when the pressure is relieved, the fluid seeps back, together with oxygen and nutrients. Hence, the health of the cartilage depends on use of the joint. Over many years, the cartilage may become frayed and may even wear away entirely. When this happens, the bone surface on one side of the joint grates against the bone on the other side of the joint, providing a much less elastic joint surface. With time, the opposing bony surfaces may become polished, a process called *eburnation*. As this happens, the joint may again move more smoothly and cause less discomfort. This is one of the reasons it is important to continue to use painful joints.

Osteoarthritis is sometimes called *osteoarthrosis*. The difference between these two terms has to do with the question of inflammation. *Itis* denotes inflammation, and with osteoarthritis very little inflammation is to be found. Hence, some experts prefer the term osteoarthrosis, which does not imply inflammation. Both words mean the same.

There are three common types of osteoarthritis. The first and mildest causes knobby enlargement of the finger joints. The end joints of the fingers become bony and the hands begin to assume the appearance we associate with old age. The other joints of the fingers may also be involved. This kind of arthritis (or arthrosis) usually causes little difficulty beyond the cosmetic. There may be some stiffness.

The second form of osteoarthritis involves the spine and is sometimes called degenerative joint disease. Bony growths (spurs) appear on the spine in the neck region or in the low back. Usually the bony growths are associated with some narrowing of the space between the vertebrae. This time the disc rather than cartilage is the material that becomes frayed. Changes in the spine begin early in life in almost all of us, but cause symptoms relatively seldom.

The third form of osteoarthritis involves the weight-bearing joints, almost always the hips and knees. These problems can be quite severe. It is possible to have all three kinds of osteoarthritis or any two of them, but often a person will have only one.

Individuals who have had fractures near a joint or have a congenital malformation at a joint seem to develop osteoarthritis in those joints at an earlier age. But, as noted, the usual description of this arthritis as "wear and tear" is not accurate. While excessive wear and tear on the joint can theoretically result in damage, activity helps the joint remain supple and lubricated, and this tends to cancel out the theoretically bad effects.

Careful studies of people who regularly put a lot of stress on joints (such as individuals who operate pneumatic drills or run long distances on hard paved surfaces) have been unable to show a relationship between these activities and the development of arthritis. Hence, intensive activity does not predispose you to arthritis any more than intensive activity predisposes you to heart disease. In fact, the very opposite may be true.

FEATURES

The bony knobs that form around the end joints of the fingers are called *Heberden's nodes* after the British doctor who first described them. In the middle joints of the fingers, similar knobs can be found. Usually, the bony enlargement occurs slowly over a period of years and is not even noticed. In most cases, all of the fingers are involved more or less equally.

Osteoarthritis of the spine does not cause symptoms unless there is pressure on one of the nerves or irritation of some of the other structures of the back. If someone tells you that you have arthritis in your spine, do not assume that the pain you feel is necessarily related to that arthritis. Most people with X-rays showing arthritis of the spine do not have any problem at all.

Osteoarthritis of the weight-bearing joints, particularly the hip and knee, develops slowly and often involves both sides of the body. Pain in the joint may remain fairly constant or may wax and wane over a period of years. In severe cases walking may be difficult or even impossible. Fluid may accumulate in the affected joint, giving it a swollen appearance, or a knee may wobble a bit when weight is placed on it. Usually, in the knee, the osteoarthritis will affect the inner or the outer half of the joint more than the other; this may result in the leg becoming bowed or splayed and may cause difficulty in walking.

X-rays can be helpful in evaluating osteoarthritis. The two major findings on the X-ray are narrowing of the joint space and the presence of bony spurs. X-rays pass right through cartilage. Hence, in a normal joint the X-ray looks as though the two bones are separated by a space. In reality, the apparent space is filled with cartilage. As the cartilage is frayed, the apparent joint space on the X-ray narrows until the two bones may touch each other. *Osteophytes*, or spurs, are little bone growths that appear alongside the places where the cartilage has degenerated. It is as though the body is trying to react to a cartilage problem by providing more surface area for the joint, so as to distribute the weight more evenly. The bony growth provides a larger joint surface, although the new bone is not covered by cartilage. In addition, X-rays can sometimes show the holes through which the nerves pass and indicate whether these holes are narrowed or not.

In contrast to X-rays, blood tests are not very helpful in diagnosing osteoarthritis. There is not anything wrong with the rest of the body, so all the tests are normal.

PROGNOSIS (THE FUTURE OF THE DISEASE)

Prognosis is good to excellent for all forms of osteoarthritis. When you think of an aging process, you tend to think of a progressive condition that will continue to get worse and worse. That is not necessarily the case. Osteoarthritis may get worse for a while and then become stable for a long time. A joint that has lost its cartilage may not function well at first, but with use the bone may be molded and polished so that a smooth and more functional joint is developed. Even in the worst cases, osteoarthritis progresses slowly. You have lots of time to think about what kinds of treatment are likely to help. If a surgical decision is needed, you can consider for some time whether you want an operation or not. Crippling from osteoarthritis is relatively rare, and most persons with osteoarthritis remain essentially free of symptoms.

TREATMENT

Joints should be exercised through their full range of motion several times a day. If weight-bearing joints are involved, body weight should be kept under control. Obesity accelerates the rate of damage. The most helpful exercises seem to be swimming, walking, and bicycling, which are easy, can be gradually increased, and are smooth rather than jerky. Exercise should be regular. Thus, if you start getting some osteoarthritis, it is not a signal to begin to tone down your life, but rather to develop a sensible regular exercise program to strengthen the bones and ligaments surrounding the affected joints and to preserve mobility in joints that are developing spurs. (For details see Chapter 7.)

Drug therapy is much less important. We use it to control the discomfort to a certain extent. Aspirin in moderate doses (or acetaminophen, such as Tylenol) is frequently helpful. Indomethacin and other anti-inflammatory drugs may be helpful for some people, particularly if the osteoarthritis is in the hip or the knee. We try to avoid codeine and other strong pain relievers because pain is a signal to the body that helps protect a diseased joint; it is important that this signal is received. (For details see Chapter 14.)

Frequently some kinds of devices can assist. A cane may be helpful; less commonly, crutches are needed. Occasionally, special shoes or lifts on one side of the foot may be helpful.

Most physicians believe that osteoarthritis may be prevented by good health habits. If you are active, maintain a lean body weight, exercise your muscles and joints regularly so as to nourish cartilage, and let your common sense tell you when you have done too much and something hurts, your joints should last a lifetime. Like exercise of the heart muscle, exercise of the muscles and joints provides reserve for the occasional strenuous activities we all encounter. Exercise builds strong tissues that last a long time.

Injection of osteoarthritic joints with corticosteroids is occasionally helpful, and sometimes removal of some fluid from a joint may help. Unfortunately, injections usually do not help much since there is not much inflammation to be suppressed. Injections should not be frequently repeated, because the injection itself may damage the cartilage and the bone.

Surgery can be dramatically effective for persons with severe osteoarthritis of the weight-bearing joints. The total hip replacement operation is the most important operation yet devised for any form of arthritis. Practically all individuals are free of pain after the surgery and many walk normally and carry out normal activities. The total knee replacement is a more recent operation that gives far better results than the knee surgery available just a few years ago. Surgery is not required on an urgent basis, and you and your doctor will want to decide the point at which the discomfort or the limitation of your walking has become sufficiently great so that the discomfort, the costs, and the small risk associated with the operation are warranted. (For more information on surgery, see Chapter 15.)

4

Osteoporosis

Osteoporosis is a disease of the bones in which the bones lose calcium and become more brittle and thus tend to break more easily. While anyone can have osteoporosis, it is most common in women after menopause. Inactivity, and sometimes the use of cortisone (prednisone) medications can greatly increase the problem. A majority of elderly individuals, especially women, have this problem. The seriousness of the disease can be seen in the fact that one in five women will break a hip before the age of 75. Thankfully, we now know of several ways to treat this disease and even prevent it. However, as with all kinds of arthritis, treatment means a daily practice of good health behaviors. The following are ways of dealing with the problem.

DIET

Calcium in the diet is very important for maintaining strong bones. For women before menopause, women taking estrogen after menopause, and for men, the daily requirement of calcium is 1,000 mg. After menopause, for women not taking estrogen, the recommendation is for 1,500 mg a day in women. There are two ways to get calcium, through what one eats and from supplementary pills.

Many foods are high in calcium. From the following chart, which shows both the calcium content and calories of common food, you can see that it is possible to get plenty of calcium from your diet.

SOURCES FOR CALCIUM

Food	Amount	Calcium (mgs)	Calories
Low-fat milk	1 cup	300	105
Whole milk	1 cup	290	161
Nonfat milk	1 cup	300	87
Nonfat milk (powdered)	1 tbsp	100	28
Almonds	2/3 cup	254	597
Yogurt (from skim milk)	1 cup	300	122
Cheddar cheese (1 inch sq.)	1 oz	200	112
Creamed cottage cheese	1 cup	200	163
Low-fat cottage cheese	1 cup	140	139
Ice cream	1 cup	200	276
Ice milk (hard)	1 cup	200	200
Salmon (canned)	4 oz	200	141
Tofu	3½ oz	100	32
Spinach	4 oz	60	31
Broccoli	1 stalk	80	21
Rhubarb (raw)	1½ cup	200	32

SUPPLEMENTAL CALCIUM

While it is good to get as much calcium as possible from your diet, sometimes it is necessary to take a calcium supplement. When buying a supplement, be sure to see how much *elemental calcium* is in each tablet. For example, a 750 mg calcium carbonate tablet contains only 300 mg of elemental calcium. Read labels carefully. Remember, you need 1,000 to 1,500 mg of elemental calcium a day. Sometimes the word *elemental* does not appear. Here are some hints. Calcium carbonate contains 40 percent elemental calcium, calcium chloride contains 36 percent, calcium lactate 13 percent, and calcium gluconate only 9 percent. Second, look at costs. One kind of calcium is pretty much like another. Therefore, don't be afraid to get less expensive products. Avoid bone meal products, which may contain lead.

Some calcium tablets contain vitamin D, which helps with calcium absorption. Other sources of vitamin D include milk and yogurt. If you live in a sunny climate such as California or Arizona, you won't need extra vitamin D. The daily requirement is only 400 units of vitamin D. Don't get carried away. This is not a case of more is better. In fact, too much vitamin D can actually *cause* bone loss.

The following chart gives you the cost of some types of calcium supplements as of summer 1986.

COST OF CALCIUM

Name	Elemental Calcium (mgs)	Price/250 mg
Oyster shell calcium (with vitamin D)	250	$0.02
Calcium carbonate	250	$0.09
Caltrate (calcium carbonate)	600	$0.05
Oscal (calcium carbonate)	500	$0.07
Oscal with vitamin D (calcium carbonate)	250	$0.07
Calcium Supplement (calcium carbonate)	300	$0.06
Tums (calcium carbonate)	200	$0.03
Calcium gluconate	93	$0.04
Calcium lactate	100	$0.10
Calcet (calcium gluconate, calcium lactate, calcium carbonate, vitamin D)	152	$0.03

It is best to take your calcium supplements spread out over the day and to take them with a little milk or yogurt. Also, take some calcium before going to bed, as more calcium is lost at night than during the day.

Here are a few tricks to help you get enough calcium:

1. Add powdered nonfat dry milk to almost anything. Every teaspoon gives you 33 mg of calcium.

2. Eat hot cereals for breakfast. This will both help your calcium intake and add bulk to your diet.

3. If you have not tried tofu, try some. You might like it.

4. Remember that fish (such as canned salmon and sardines) that has been prepared with its bones has a high amount of calcium.

MYTHS ABOUT CALCIUM

1. **"Calcium causes bone spurs."** No, bone spurs are caused by loss of cartilage and growth of new bone; they have nothing to do with calcium intake in the diet.

2. **"Foods high in calcium are fattening."** Some high calcium foods such as whole milk and ice cream are also high in calories. However, many high calcium foods such as nonfat milk, vegetables, and salmon are low in calories. One does not need to avoid calcium, only foods that are high in fat.

3. **"Calcium causes kidney stone."** If calcium intake is under 2,000 mg per day, this shouldn't be a concern for most people. However, if you have ever had kidney stones, it is a good idea to talk with your physician before taking large amounts of calcium.

4. **"Calcium causes constipation."** To some extent this is true. However, by taking plenty of fluids and eating foods high in fiber, you can avoid this problem. See Chapter 13 for more information.

SALT

Salt is bad for osteoporosis. The problem is not really salt but sodium, the main ingredient in salt. When the body has too much sodium, the sodium is excreted in the urine, and at the same time, calcium is excreted. Thus, a low-sodium diet is good for osteoporosis. It is also important for maintaining a low blood pressure. By limiting your sodium, you can't lose.

To test yourself on your knowledge of which foods are high in sodium, rank the following list. Give a 10 to the food highest in sodium and a 1 to the item with the least sodium. Check your answer on page 24.

SODIUM EXERCISE

carrot	orange
cheese, cheddar (2 oz)	pickle, dill
cheese, processed (2 oz)	pies, most types (1/6)
chicken, cooked (3 oz)	potato chips (10 large)
frankfurter	tuna in oil (3/4 cup)

HORMONES

The use of hormones after menopause has long been a topic of controversy. This is a subject every woman should discuss with her physician. The following discussion is to help you understand some of the issues.

There are two female hormones, estrogen and progestin. These hormones are normally created during the menstrual cycle. However, after menopause, their levels fall greatly. Taking supplemental estrogen after menopause seems to protect against osteoporosis. However, it is believed by some to increase the likelihood of endometrial cancer (cancer of the lining of the uterus). However, when progesterone is taken with the estrogen, this risk is greatly reduced and the prevention of osteoporosis is increased. The decision to take no hormone, one hormone (estrogen, progestin), or a combination of the two is a personal one that should be discussed with a physician. The correct treatment is still very much in debate.

EXERCISE

Weight-bearing exercise is most important to keeping strong bones. The body reacts to such exercise by increasing the calcium content and thus the strength of the bones. Walking is the best example. If at all possible, walk half a mile to a mile a day. Even if this is unrealistic for you, remember that even a little weight-bearing exercise is important. Do as much as you can. For suggestions on developing a walking program, see pages 83–84. Recent research has shown that women need to walk 4 miles a week to get maximal exercise benefit for osteoporosis prevention. This includes all the walking we do in our daily lives. (Note: Swimming is *not* a weight-bearing exercise.)

ACCIDENT PREVENTION

Unfortunately, it is not always possible to prevent osteoporosis or undo damage already done. Thus, accident avoidance is very important to prevent broken bones. The following are a few hints:

- Avoid throw rugs — they are slippery and have a bad habit of tripping the unwary.

- Be sure all stairs have a secure railing that is easy to grasp.

- If advised by a health professional, use a cane or walker. Don't be ashamed; these can be real bone savers.

- Even if you don't usually use a cane, consider using one for getting up at night. This is a time when most of us may be easily unbalanced and a cane can help prevent bad spills.

- Watch for uneven walks, curbs, floors, etc.

- Move the phone to a convenient place so you won't trip over the cord.

- Wear shoes that give good support.

- Use step stools that are stable and in good repair.

- Use nonskid mats in the bathroom, shower, and on the bathroom floor. Permanently install grab bars to wall or edge of tub.

- If you are unsteady on your feet, use a stool with nonskid feet, when showering or bathing.

- Have light switches at the top and bottom of all stairs.

In summary, there are four things you can do to help prevent and treat osteoporosis.

1. Do some weight-bearing exercises daily.

2. Using diet or a combination of diet and supplements, take 1,000 to 1,500 mg of elemental calcium daily.

3. If advised by your physician, take estrogen, progestin, or a combination of these hormones.

4. Make your home and other surroundings accident safe.

SODIUM EXERCISE ANSWER SHEET

pickle	10	1200 mg sodium
tuna	9	800 mg
cheese, processed	8	700 mg
frankfurter	7	550 mg
pie	6	425 mg
cheese, cheddar	5	360 mg
potato chips	4	250 mg
chicken	3	80 mg
carrot	2	30 mg
orange	1	1 mg

5

Those Nagging Pains
Bursitis, Fibrositis, and Getting Old

Most of the problems we tend to call arthritis don't even involve the joint and really aren't even diseases. This is good news. Painful local conditions involving only one or two parts of the body are almost always just an irritation or injury of that part. After that part is rested or fixed everything is all right again. There is no crippling, no threat to life, no need for dangerous medications. Remember the basic principle: For a local problem use a local treatment. Very seldom will you want to take a medication by mouth for a pain in, say, an elbow.

There are a lot of names for these conditions — bursitis, low back strain, sciatica, metatarsalgia, Achilles tendinitis, heel-spur syndrome, sprained ankle, cervical neck strain, frozen shoulder, tennis elbow, housemaid's knee, carpal-tunnel syndrome, and others. Many people call all of these bursitis, while doctors have other and fancier names for them. But they all are local conditions and are approached the same way. At first you don't even need a doctor for them, but if they don't respond after six weeks of self-treatment or seem alarmingly severe, be sure to see the doctor.

BURSITIS

A bursa is a small sac of tissue similar to the synovial tissue that lines the joints. The bursa sac contains a lubricating fluid, and the bursa is designed to ease the movement of muscle across muscle or of muscle across bone. A bursa does not connect to the joint space of the nearby joint but is a separate sac. In the grand scheme of things the bursa is just an annoying little body area, but bursae can be very painful when they become inflamed. Usually, only one or two will be inflamed at a time, but bursitis of over 20 bursae can occur, and the problems can come and go over the years.

"Housemaid's knee" is a popular term for *prepatellar bursitis,* in which the bursa in front and just below the kneecap is inflamed. *Olecranon bursitis* occurs over the point of the elbow, and sometimes a fluid-filled sac is visible at that point. *Subdeltoid bursitis* occurs at the shoulder, or more precisely, on the outer aspect of the upper arm just below the shoulder.

Features

Bursitis is inflammation of a bursa and results in localized pain. Sometimes the pain is on both sides of the body, as with both knees. There is pain when the inflamed area is pressed, and heat and redness are common. If the bursa is located close enough to the skin, swelling can be seen. Many bursae, however, are buried deep between muscles.

Bursitis comes on relatively suddenly, from within hours to days. It frequently follows injury to the area, repeated pressure on the area, or overuse. In the shoulders, particularly, it may be associated with inflammation of the tendon and can be part of a "frozen shoulder" problem.

Prognosis

Almost all episodes of bursitis will subside from within several days to several weeks, but may recur. If the process causing the bursitis is continued, the bursitis may persist, otherwise it follows a normal healing course over a period of from one week to ten days. Some people seem more prone to bursitis than others and have recurrent problems throughout their lives. If the affected part is held rigid, some permanent stiffness may result; otherwise no crippling whatsoever should result from bursitis.

Treatment

If the problem is tolerable, treat it with "tincture of time." Wait for the body to control and heal the process. Avoid the precipitating cause. Use drugs very sparingly; the process is local and systemic drugs like aspirin are not very helpful. Resting the part will speed the healing, and you may want to use a sling or other device to increase the rest. Gentle warmth provided by a heating pad or warm bath frequently makes the bursitis feel better. The affected area should be worked through its full range of motion two to four times a day, even if it is a bit tender, to prevent stiffness from developing. Additional techniques described in Chapter 8 may also be helpful. But remember, patience and avoidance of reinjury are the major tactics.

If the discomfort persists for a number of weeks despite the measures outlined above, see the doctor. Often, the doctor will recommend that you continue the same general measures discussed here. Alternatively, an anti-inflammatory drug may be prescribed; these help few people and are generally just a way of buying a little more patience from the patient. Finally, the doctor may inject the bursa with corticosteroids (see Chapter 14). These injections are usually successful and not overly painful. They are relatively free of side effects and most physicians feel that they are appropriate treatment for a local condition that is severe and persistent.

FIBROSITIS

Features

Fibrositis is a condition of widespread aches and pains which is very common but has only been recognized recently. People with arthritis often have a "fibrositic component" to their arthritis, and this is often relatively easy to treat, although pain medication does not help.

Prognosis

Fibrositis involves minor injuries of the muscles and joints, together with tension and stress. The muscles stay tense throughout the day and often even when you are asleep. This puts extra strain on the ligaments and results in pain, often severe and persistent for many months. Sleep is often disturbed. Points in the muscle or over the ligaments can be very sore when pressure is applied.

Treatment

The key to management of fibrositis is increased physical activity, together with relaxation techniques. The self-management techniques described in the next chapters are designed to help with any fibrositis problems you may have, as well as with arthritis.

GETTING OLD

Local injuries, like bursitis, are often dismissed as "just getting old, I guess." It is true that more older people than younger people have these problems, and they do have something to do with the way that our bodies age.

But they do not need to happen. These problems are sometimes due to abuse of a body part, as in prepatellar bursitis from scrubbing floors on your knees. Much more frequently, however, they are due to disuse. In our society, as you get older you are expected to be less active. And then you get the kinds of health problems that happen to inactive people of all ages. The relationship between local problems and age is mostly accidental; it is really an association of local problems with inactivity.

So you need to be active. If your muscles are trim and in good tone, your heart and lungs are conditioned, your body weight is normal and constant at that level, and you have a regular exercise program, you will have far fewer of these problems, and your body will not grow old as rapidly. These measures will keep calcium in your bones, your bursae free and well lubricated, your tendons firm and strong, and your joint cartilage well nourished.

You can control a lot of the aging of your body. The worst mistake that you can make is to consider bursitis or another local problem to be a signal to slow down. It is a signal to speed up, because your body is drifting out of condition. In Chapter 7 we go through some of the exercises that will help.

6

Becoming an Arthritis Self-Manager

Self-management seems like a simple enough term. Yet, it needs some explaining. Both at home and in the business world the managers direct the show. They don't do everything themselves, they work with others, including consultants, to get the job done. What makes them unique is that they are responsible for making the decisions and making sure that these decisions are carried through. As an arthritis self-manager, your job is much the same. You gather information from friends, family, the Arthritis Foundation, and written materials. You hire a consultant or a team of consultants, your physician, physical therapist, pharmacists, and other health professionals. Once they have given you their best advice, it is up to you to follow through.

Being a good manager means working with others, discussing problems and, most important, understanding that the follow-through is up to you. This doesn't mean that all your decisions will be correct. Managing arthritis, like managing a family, is a complex undertaking. There are many twists, turns, and midcourse corrections. By learning self-management skills you can ease the problems of living with arthritis.

The key to success in any undertaking is first learning a set of skills and then practicing them until they have been mastered. Children cannot read before first learning to recognize the letters of the alphabet. They then learn the sounds of combinations of letters. Later, they learn the meanings of simple words and phrases. It is only after years of practice and mastery that one is able to read a novel. Think about it. The same is true with almost everything we do, from baking a cake to driving a car to planting a garden. These tasks are all based on learning skills and mastering them. Success in arthritis self-management is the same. One needs to learn a set of skills and then to practice them daily until success is reached. This book is full of skills that can help relieve some of the problems caused by arthritis. However, we have learned that knowing the skills is not enough. Most of us need a way of incorporating these skills into our daily lives. Unfortunately, whenever we try a new skill, the first attempts are clumsy, slow, and show few results. It is easier to return to our old ways than to continue to try to master new and sometimes difficult skills. One of the best ways to master new skills is through goal setting. In the following pages, we will try to outline some of the principles of goal setting. If you use these principles, the success of an arthritis self-management program is almost assured.

GOALS

Long-Term Goals

There are two types of goals, long-term and short-term. An example of a long-term goal is wanting to play golf, pick up our children or grandchildren, or walk a mile. Most of us are pretty good at naming our long-term goals. The question to ask yourself is "What would I like to do that I am unable to do because of my arthritis?" Take a few moments and write your long-term goals in the space below.

Long-term goals:

1. _____

2. _____

3. _____

Long-term goals are important because they set an objective. However, they are little help in achieving successful skill mastery. To do this, one needs to work on short-term goals.

A short-term goal is just what it says, a goal to be accomplished today or, at most, this week. Short-term goals are the steps to achieving a long-term goal. Examples of short-term goals might be: "Today, I will do two strengthening exercises for my knees"; or "Today, I will do six stretching exercises for my shoulder"; or "Today, I will walk around the block." As you can see, these short-term goals relate to the long-term goals but demand a specific action *now!*

Since short-term goals are so important, let us now look at them more carefully.

Short-Term Goals

First, a short-term goal must call for a *specific* action that you can *realistically* expect to accomplish now. Most of us can do things that would make us healthier but often fail to do them. For example, most people with arthritis can walk. Some just across a room, others half a block, most can walk several blocks, and some can walk a mile or more. However, we seldom do this even though we know it is good for us. Therefore, a short-term goal might be to walk around the block four times this week.

By being specific, we mean that a goal must have the following parts:

1. **An action.** Do something, such as walk, exercise, call a friend, take a medication, or lose weight.

2. **Description.** This gives the detail so anyone listening to or reading your goal would be able to know exactly what you mean. The description always includes at least one of the following:

   a. **What kind?** For example, instead of "exercise" you might be more specific by saying, "stretching exercise of my shoulder."

   b. **How far, how much, how many?** For example, instead of "walk," you might say "walk around the block"; or instead of "stretching exercise of the shoulder," you might say "three stretching exercises of the shoulder."

3. **How often?** This is the final part of the goal but again, must be so specific that anyone reading or listening to your goal would be able to know exactly what you expect to do. For example, instead of "walk around the block once a day," you might say "walk around the block four times this week after lunch."

Thus, a goal must:

1. Have an *action*

2. Give *details* about the action

3. Describe *how often* the action will be done

Earlier, we said that a short-term goal must be both specific and realistic. The above discussion should help you be specific. Being realistic is just as important. Goals should be set in such a way that they can be accomplished fairly easily. On the other hand, they should require some change in your behavior. For example, if you never eat after dinner, setting a goal of not eating after dinner may be specific but will accomplish nothing, as it requires no behavior change.

A good test of reality is to ask yourself, on a scale of 1 to 10, "How certain am I that I can accomplish this goal this week?"

1	2	3	4	5	6	7	8	9	10
	Very			Moderately				Very	
	uncertain			certain				certain	

If you answer 9 or 10, very certain, the goal may be too easy and you might think about making it a bit more challenging. On the other hand, if you answer 1, 2, or 3, your goal may be too difficult and you should be a bit easier on yourself.

Where most people have problems is that they make the goals too difficult. It is either too big or it is done too often. It is best to give yourself some room to slip. The best goals are those that you accomplish. This in turn helps you set more goals. One of the best examples of this type of goal setting is Alcoholics Anonymous. Members do not set the goal of never drinking; rather, the goal is not to drink today.

In setting short-term goals for arthritis, there are a couple of rules that may help you toward success.

1. **Start where you are or start slowly.** If you can now walk around the block, start your walking program with walking around the block not with walking a mile. If you have never done any exercises for arthritis, start by doing only two or three repetitions a day for only one

or two joints. If you want to lose weight, set a goal based on your eating behaviors, such as not eating after dinner. See Chapter 7 for help in starting an exercise program and Chapter 13 for more information on dieting and nutrition.

2. **Give yourself some time off.** All people have days when they don't feel like doing anything. Therefore, it is best to say that you will do something three to five times a week but not every day. That way if you don't feel like walking one day, you can still meet your goal. In review, there are five guides for goal setting.

1. Choose an action.

2. Give specific details about the action, such as what kind, how far, how much, how many, when, and where.

3. Decide how often you will do whatever you decide.

4. Start where you are.

5. Give yourself some time off.

Now that you know about short-term goals, write one or two short-term goals that will help you reach your long-term goals.

Short-term goals:

1. _____

2. _____

3. _____

4. _____

5. _____

The following page is an example of a goal sheet. It will help you keep track of your daily progress. Make a copy and put it on your refrigerator door or somewhere you will see it several times a day. Filling out your daily progress is a good way of beginning to reach your long-term goal. To really become a skillful goal setter, keep weekly goal sheets for at least six weeks.

WEEKLY GOAL CHART

Long-term Goal:								
Weekly Goals	1	2	3	4	5	6	7	Notes
1								Accomplishments: Problems:
2								Accomplishments: Problems:
3								Accomplishments: Problems:

1. Write your long-term goal across the top.
2. Write your weekly goals in the left column.
3. Daily check the goals you accomplish.
4. At the end of the week, note your accomplishments and problems in the far right column.

Now that you know how to set goals, the next trick to being a good self-manager is to get help in accomplishing your goals.

Ask family or friends to check with you on how you are doing. Having to report your progress is good motivation. Also, if you run into problems, don't stop; get help. For example, one self-manager we know was going to walk with a co-worker every day at lunch. The problem was that even though the co-worker tried to slow down, she walked too fast. The solution was simple. The woman asked her co-worker to always walk slightly behind her. Thus, the self-manager set the pace and was able to continue her daily walk.

Another self-manager wanted to tell her grown children that hosting big holiday dinners had just become too much for her. However, she didn't know how to do this. By talking to friends, she first decided to offer to cook the turkey and have the children each bring a dish and clean up. Then, she rehearsed saying, "I know how much of a tradition holiday dinners are. However, I just can't do as much anymore. I'll cook the turkey, and will you each bring something?" This story had a happy ending, as the children had all wanted to help for years but had not offered for fear of offending their mother. Chapter 9 can help you with problem solving.

For some problems, consultants can be helpful. If medications are causing problems, ask the advice of your physician. If you just stop taking the drug, you are cheating yourself in two ways. First, you are not getting the benefits of medication. Second, you have not supplied your consultant with the vital information he or she needs to help you manage successfully.

If you really enjoy swimming, but have problems because you cannot comfortably turn your head, check with an occupational therapist. You probably don't need ongoing treatment, but one problem-solving visit with a professional may keep you in the water. (In this case the solution was a face mask and snorkel.)

The best part of being a good self-manager is the rewards you will get in accomplishing your goals. However, don't wait till your goal's attained; reward yourself frequently. For example, decide that you won't read the paper until after you exercise. Thus, reading the paper becomes your reward. One self-manager we know buys only one or two pieces of fruit at a time and walks the half-mile to the supermarket every day or two to get more fruit. Rewards don't have to be fancy or expensive, just something that is pleasant and meaningful in your life.

In review, a successful arthritis self-manager:

1. Sets long-term goals.

2. Sets short-term goals.

3. Uses friends and family to help accomplish goals.

4. Utilizes friends, family, and consultants to solve problems when they arise.

5. Rewards oneself frequently for accomplishing short-term goals.

7

Use It or Lose It
Exercises for
Your Arthritis

*my problem is
my right knee
#20
2 × per day
do it 5 times.
5 times a week.*

0 |_____75'_____| 100

*Do relaxation
P- 97*

One of the most important things you can do to help your arthritis is to exercise, if you do it right. Unfortunately, many people with arthritis think exercise is harmful. Others become discouraged because progress is slow or their exercises are painful. Maintaining a proper balance between rest and exercise and exercising properly are the keys to a successful arthritis exercise program. Let us examine the benefits of exercise, some basic principles, and the different types of exercise. With this knowledge you can plan a successful and enjoyable program.

BENEFITS OF EXERCISE

There are numerous benefits of exercise, touching many aspects of our physical and psychological lives. It is well known that exercise leads to increased strength and flexibility in the muscles and ligaments surrounding the joints. In addition, research has shown that exercise helps to maintain or increase the strength of bone. More active forms of exercise, such as swimming or walking, have important effects on the heart that promote increased endurance and circulation and fight

37

deterioration of the arteries. In addition, even small amounts of these exercises will help you avoid constipation and overcome fatigue.

Every tissue in the body requires certain foods or nutrients to work effectively. Most tissues have arteries that bring essential foods to them, but this is not true of the joint cartilage. It is only through movement that nourishment is brought by the synovial fluid to the joint cartilage and that waste products are removed. Thus, exercise promotes good joint nutrition.

An appropriate exercise program can lead to a general sense of well-being and accomplishment. It is easy to feel good about yourself when you are accomplishing the goals of a realistic exercise program. Further, the social interactions encouraged by many forms of exercise are also rewarding.

Exercise is a way we can prevent the loss of function that may accompany arthritis. There is a saying that applies particularly to persons with arthritis: "Use it or lose it." If you do not use a muscle or joint, you will lose strength and mobility, and thus, function. If loss of function has already occurred, it is important to remember that it was not lost in one day. Likewise, it cannot be regained in one day. Slow progress is to be expected, particularly if your arthritis is severe or your joint limitations have existed for a long time. Expect some setbacks in any exercise program, but keep at it. Your efforts will be rewarded in many ways.

TYPES OF EXERCISE

There are three basic types of exercise. **Range-of-motion** or **stretching exercises** involve moving a joint as far as it will comfortably go (through its full range of motion) and then coaxing it a little farther, just past the point of beginning pain or discomfort. These exercises are designed to increase and then maintain joint mobility, thus decreasing pain and improving function.

Strengthening exercises increase muscle strength and thus lend stability to vulnerable joints. They improve your ability to bear weight, lift objects, and sustain movement. Strengthening exercises should be done in such a way as to minimize stress on the joints. For this reason, good strengthening exercises are *isometric*. These exercises involve use (contraction) of a muscle or muscles without movement at the joint. Discussion and examples of the isometric principle can be found in the section on specific strengthening exercises. Remember, strengthening exercises are not a substitute for stretching exercises. They will not increase joint range of motion.

Endurance exercises are necessary because neither stretching nor strengthening exercises will increase your endurance. More active forms of exercise, such as walking, swimming, bicycling, jogging, danc-ing, or cross-country skiing will promote cardiovascular fitness. In-clude some kind of active exercise in your program every day, but re-member to start out easily and progress slowly. To help reduce stress while walking or dancing wear low-heeled, rubber-soled, lightweight shoes.

Ideally, an exercise program should include all three types of ex-ercise. Strengthening exercises are good for all joints, stretching exer-cises are particularly helpful if there is limitation of motion, and en-durance exercise helps both the joints and your overall health.

PRINCIPLES OF EXERCISE

When Should I Exercise?

Exercises should be done daily for the rest of your life. It is the "week-end warrior" who gets into trouble with painful strained muscles and ligaments. The only time a joint should not be exercised is when it is inflamed, or "hot" (swollen, red, tender to the touch). The "hot" joint is one of the special exercise considerations for people with rheuma-toid arthritis. However, even those hot joints should be gently moved through the full range of motion twice a day.

Find a specific time and place to exercise and make this a part of your daily routine. You will have to decide on the best time, but con-sider the following: It is best to exercise when (1) you have the least pain, (2) you have the least stiffness, (3) you are not tired, and (4) your medication is having maximal effect. You probably want one such pe-riod early in the day, and one later.

What Can I Do to Prepare for Exercise?

Athletes learn that warming up before exercise means a more produc-tive session and helps prevent injuries. Here are some warm-up suggestions.

1. A nice, slow general stretch: Lying in bed, (a) stretch one arm up and then the other, (b) push arms forward, opening hands wide, (c) pull arms back and close hands, (d) pull knees up and do a few bicycle turns in the air, (e) stretch legs out straight, (f) roll to the side, swinging legs off the edge of the bed, using momentum to help you sit up. This warm-up is helpful when first getting up in the morning and is very similar to what a cat does as it gets up from a rest.

2. Begin your exercise program with small movements in a pain-free range. These movements can be anything from your chosen exercise

done less vigorously to a good shake (like a dog shaking). Before walking or jogging do some gentle stretching of the leg muscles.

3. Massage can be used to relax stiff joints and muscles prior to exercise. However, it is best not to deeply massage a "hot" joint.

4. Apply heat prior to exercise. Heat tends to relax joints and muscles and relieve pain. How you apply the heat is up to you. No way is better than another. You do not need special equipment or mineral waters. All of the following are acceptable ways of applying heat. When using heat always test carefully for temperature (the elbow is a good tester) to avoid burns. Limit your use of heat to 20 minutes at a time.

   a. Take a long, hot bath. A hot spring, whirlpool bath, or hot tub is nice, but not necessary. Use caution and stand up slowly as the heat sometimes causes dizziness.

   b. Take a long, hot shower and aim the full force of the water at the painful joint(s). Hand-held showers with a massage unit can be pleasant.

   c. An electric heating pad can be placed over the affected area. Be sure the hot pad has a cover and that you do not fall asleep with it plugged in. It is best not to lie directly on the pad, and never use an electric pad with anything wet.

   d. Fill a hot-water bottle with hot water. Be sure it is not hot enough to burn you. Again, it is best not to lie directly on the water bottle.

   e. Stand next to your heater or radiator.

5. If you don't get good results from heat, the application of cold may prove more effective, especially for the "hot" joint of rheumatoid arthritis. Cold relaxes muscles and produces a numbing effect, thus decreasing pain and increasing joint motion. As with heat, there are a few important principles of application:

   a. If you are especially sensitive to cold or have decreased sensation or circulation such as in Raynaud's Disease or vasculitis, do not apply cold. Ask your doctor or therapist if you are unsure.

   b. Apply just long enough to achieve a numbing effect — no more than 15 to 20 minutes.

   c. Be cautious when exercising after applying cold; the numbing effect may allow you to overdo. Remember, if the joint is "hot," restrict exercise to moving the joint through its full range of motion twice a day.

   d. Place the cold pack over the joint, not between the joint and a firm surface.

e. Check during and after application for any sign of a break in the skin.

Cold packs can be bought, or you can create your own. Wrapping the pack in a warm, moist towel will help you adjust to the cold. Use whichever cold pack method is easiest and most effective for you:

a. Several resourceful people have suggested a sack of frozen peas! You can refreeze it and use it again.
b. Massage with a large ice cube.
c. Make a slush pack: Line a bowl with two heavy plastic bags; fill with three cups water and one cup denatured alcohol. Fasten the bags and place the bowl in the freezer until slush forms. You can refreeze a slush pack.

How Should I Exercise?

Be consistent and stick to your chosen set of exercises. Begin at a comfortable level for you and gradually increase the number of repetitions. Progress more slowly with rheumatoid joints that are prone to "hot" periods. With this gradual progression you will avoid unnecessary pain.

Your exercises should minimize stress on the affected joints. Carefully assess the stress each exercise imposes on the priority joint and those surrounding it. You will find further discussion of this throughout the chapter.

Exercises for arthritis should be performed with a slow, steady rhythm. Give your muscles time to relax between repetitions of each exercise (10 to 15 seconds). After a muscle is used, it must relax and lengthen so that waste products of muscle action can be carried away. Learning to relax readily and completely during exercise will make any exercise program more effective and enjoyable. Techniques aimed at release of residual tension throughout the body will be discussed in Chapter 8.

It is important to coordinate your breathing with exercise. Breathe deeply and rhythmically as you exercise; never hold your breath. Interspersing deep breathing with exercise ensures an adequate oxygen supply to working muscles as well as release of tension. Deep breathing involves inhaling slowly and gently through your nose and drawing air down into your abdomen. Hold for at least five counts. Exhale slowly and gently through lightly closed lips for at least five counts. You can do this breathing exercise in between the exercises described later.

What Should I Avoid?

Remember that your exercises should minimize stress on the joints. Avoid high-tension exercises such as weightlifting. If your weight-bearing joints are affected (hips, knees, ankles, or spine), jogging and such activities as aerobic dance should be approached cautiously. Bicycling for a painful knee should also be approached with caution: set a stationary bicycle on the lowest resistance or use a low gear on a conventional bicycle.

If a chosen exercise for one joint places excessive stress on another involved joint — for example, a shoulder exercise that stresses an involved hand, or a hip exercise that stresses a painful low back — modify the exercise or substitute another.

As stated earlier, avoid exercising the hot, inflamed joint, but remember to move it through its full range of motion twice a day. Deep massage of the painful joint should also be avoided. Never take extra medication to mask joint pain before exercising. This could result in joint damage, as pain is your real guide to when you've done too much.

Since warmth helps relax stiff muscles and joints, avoid becoming chilled during exercise. Wear warm clothing and do not exercise in a draft or a cold room. Hand exercises can be done in a basin of warm water.

When Have I Done Too Much?

Use common sense and listen to the signals your body gives you. A general rule of thumb is that if *exercise-induced pain lasts longer than two hours, cut back. Do not stop.* The key here is "exercise-induced." If you do your exercises and then go out and garden for three hours, the chances are that the prolonged gardening is responsible for any residual pain.

Any exercise program is bound to have setbacks, but these are not permanent. If you experience exercise-induced pain for longer than two hours, decrease the number of repetitions or be less forceful. If that does not help, choose a different exercise that will achieve the same result but that is more appropriate for you. Also, review the principles of exercise discussed here and in the sections on stretching, strengthening, and endurance exercises.

STRETCHING, OR RANGE-OF-MOTION, EXERCISES

The general rule for stretching exercises is to move the joint as far as it will comfortably go (its full range of motion) and then coax it a little farther, just past the point of first pain. Do not "bounce." A gentle, sustained stretch will be less stressful to your joints and more effective. **Each stretching exercise should be repeated three to ten times, two to four times a day, depending on pain.** Remember one of the basic principles of exercise as you decide on the number of repetitions — start slowly and easily. Again, if you have exercise-induced pain lasting longer than two hours, cut back a little. Don't give up.

The exercises in this section are examples of stretching exercises. As you become familiar with the principles involved, you may want to design your own exercises or incorporate others you have learned.

Before proceeding to the exercises, take a mental survey of your joints. To maintain your present function, you must move every joint in your body through its full range of motion every day. This movement usually occurs during your daily activities. However, because of your arthritis you may be protecting some joints by not moving them. Do you have joints that are not moved through their full range of motion every day or joints that you cannot move as far as you used to? If so, please list them here.

1. _____ *knees* _____
2. _____ *hips* _____
3. _____ *back* _____

In the following chart, you will find a list of daily activities matched with numbers for the exercises in this chapter. If you are having trouble with any of these activities, you may find it useful to focus on the exercises that correspond to them.

Once you have reached your goal for one of the joints you have trouble with, you can then add stretching exercises for another. But remember, to maintain the mobility that you worked so hard to achieve you must move that joint through its full range of motion once or twice a day. If you notice that you are losing ground with that joint, then resume a more concentrated stretching program.

Now, turn to the appropriate stretching exercises for your priority joints.

HANDS

The hand is a very delicate and intricate part of the body. The following exercises will help maintain or increase movements essential to the skilled movements we perform with our hands. If you have severe hand deformity or involvement, you may wish to consult an occupational or

Activities	Exercise Numbers
Dressing and Grooming:	
Dress yourself	1–6, 8–14, 27, 35–36, 39–42, 50–51
Upper half	15–16, 19–25, 29, 33, 43–49
Lower half	4–6, 8–14
Shampoo your hair	4–6, 8–14
Arising	
Stand up from armless chair	16, 19–20, 22, 33, 43, 45–48, 52–53
Get in and out of bed	30, 32, 33, 40, 44–45, 47–49, 52–53
Eating	
Cut your meat	1–9, 35–39, 42
Lift a full cup	1–9, 35–39, 42
Open a new milk carton	1–8, 35–39
Walking	
Walk outdoors on flat ground	15–18, 20–22, 43–49, 52–53
Climb stairs	16, 20–21, 23–25, 44–49
Hygiene	
Wash and dry your body	2, 5–6, 8–10, 12–16, 20, 29–30, 39, 42, 45, 47, 52–53
Take a tub bath	16, 20–21, 42–43, 47–48, 52–53
Get on and off toilet	16, 20–21, 42–43, 47–48, 52–53
Reach	
Reach 5 lb. object from overhead	2–6, 8–14, 35–42
Bend down to floor and lift 5 lb. object	2–6, 8–10, 13, 16, 20–22, 39–49
Grip	
Open car doors	1–12, 35–36, 38–42
Open jars	1–8, 35–39
Turn faucets on and off	1–8, 35–39
Errands	
Get in and out of car	1–6, 8–13, 16, 19–22, 24–25, 27, 29–30, 35–36, 38–53

physical therapist in developing your initial program. Also, when choosing exercises for other parts of the body, remember to assess the stress imposed on the hands and modify the exercise if necessary. See Chapter 9 for suggestions on how to modify activities to protect the involved hand.

1. One-Two-Three Finger Exercise

For optimum function you should be able to touch the tips of your fingers to the palm. When stretching the fingertips toward the palm use the "one-two-three" approach. Begin with the joint closest to the tip of the finger (A), then move on to the middle joint (B). When your fingertips are touching the palm or as close as possible, bend the knuckle joint (C). You may exercise your fingers individually or together, using your other hand to guide the movement if necessary.

A   B   C

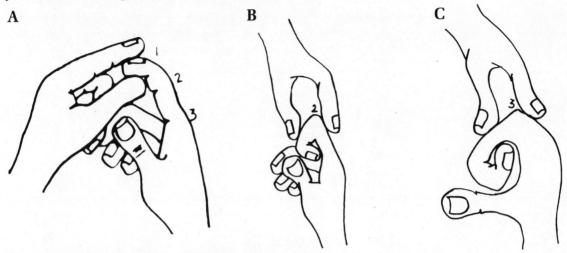

2. Three-Two-One Finger Exercise

If any of the joints in your fingers will not straighten completely, try this exercise, which is the reverse of 1. With your fingertips as close to the palm as possible, begin to uncurl your hand. Begin with the knuckle joint (A), move to the middle joint (B), and finally exercise the joint closest to the tip of the finger (C).

A   B   C

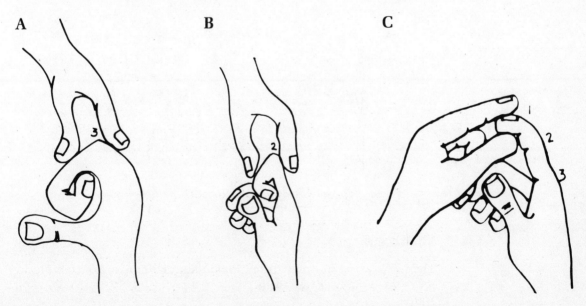

3. Fingers Flat Exercise

This is another exercise for straightening the joints of the fingers. Lay your hand as flat as possible on a table. Place the heel of your other hand across your fingers and gently press down, straightening the fingers.

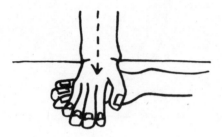

4. The Thumb Walk

Try to form a letter "O" with each attempt of this exercise. Lightly touch the tip of the thumb to the tip of the index finger (A), then spread your fingers as wide as you can (B). Proceed on to touch the tip of the thumb to the tips of your other fingers, spreading the fingers wide after each attempt. If you cannot quite bring the thumb to touch the finger, use the other hand to coax them closer together.

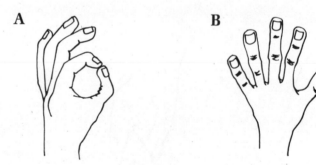

WRISTS

The next two exercises will help maintain or improve your ability to move the wrist back and forth.

5. The Palm Press

First, place your hands together, palms touching and fingers slightly entwined (A). Press the right hand backward with the left hand (B), then reverse and press the left hand backward with the right hand. Exert pressure at the palm, not the fingertips. Coax the hand just past the point of discomfort.

A　　　　　　　　　　　　　　B

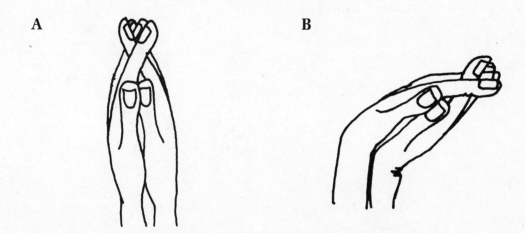

6. Wrist Table Stretch

For a more vigorous wrist stretch hang the hand over the edge of a table or arm rest with the palm down. Raise the hand up as far as possible, using your other hand to assist with the stretch (A). Then lower the hand, stretching just past the point of discomfort (B).

A　　　　　　　　　　　　　　B

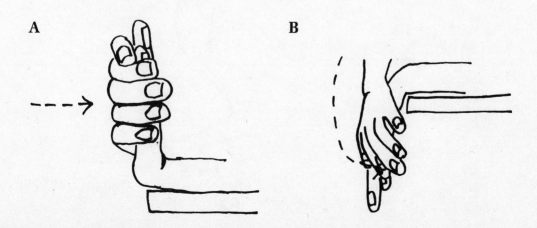

7. The Slide

If you notice that your fingers drift toward the little finger side of the hand (a common deformity in rheumatoid arthritis), this exercise is for you. Place your forearm on a table, palm down. Slide each finger toward the thumb, not moving the forearm. Use your other hand to assist if necessary. Repeat with the other hand. The exercise works to keep your knuckles and wrist in correct alignment with your forearm, promoting optimal function.

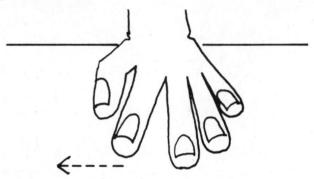

8. The Door Opener

This is an exercise to stretch the muscles and ligaments that rotate the forearm, allowing you to turn doorknobs and unlock doors. Start with your forearm resting on a table, palm down. Turn your hand so the palm faces up. If you use your other hand to assist with the stretch, grasp the lower part of the forearm, *not* the hand.

PALM UP

ELBOWS

9. The Elbow Chop

The diagonal pattern in this exercise is similar to that of chopping wood and is designed to help you bend and straighten the elbow completely. Place hands together and bend both elbows until your hands touch your right shoulder (A). Then bring hands down to touch the left knee, straightening elbows completely (B). Remember to coax the elbow a little farther than it wants to go. Reverse directions, going from left shoulder to right knee.

A
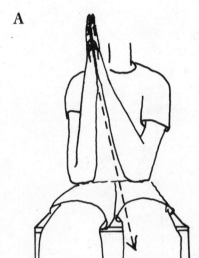

B
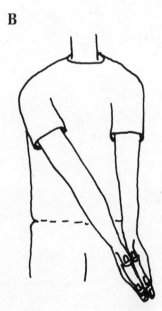

SHOULDERS

The shoulder is one of those joints that moves in many directions. When choosing stretching exercises, it is important to decide which functions are most important to you.

10. The Pendulum

This exercise is good as the beginning exercise for the very painful or limited shoulder. It facilitates relaxation of the shoulder muscles as well as free joint movement in all directions. From a standing or sitting position, lean slightly forward. Let your arm hang freely in front of you. Relax and feel the weight of your arm. Keeping the arm straight, begin with small circles and gradually increase their size. Remember to exercise to just past the point of discomfort. Don't get carried away with your circles.

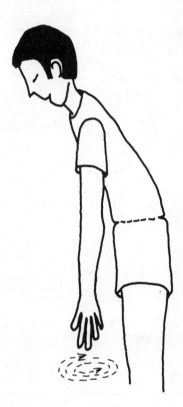

11. The Shoulder Rotator

If you have difficulty touching the back of your neck, combing your hair, or zipping a back zipper, then you probably need to work on outward rotation of the shoulder. Here are two ways to accomplish this movement. (A) Clasp your hands together at the back of your neck and pull the elbows as far back as possible. You should feel a stretch at the front of the shoulder and chest. (B) If you are not yet ready for the first exercise, begin with this method. Hold your arm close to your side with elbow bent. Keeping elbow at your side, rotate hand and forearm outward as far away from your stomach as possible. You may use your other hand to assist with the stretch. This exercise may be easier if you do it while you're lying on your back.

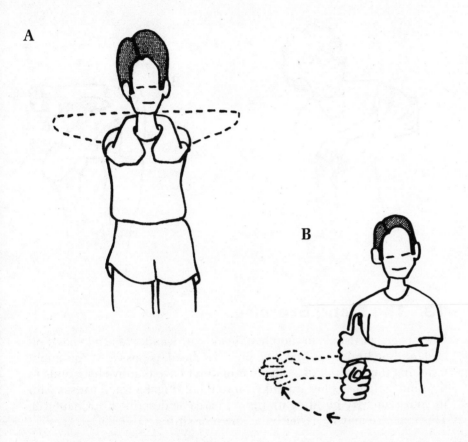

A

B

Here are three exercises to increase your ability to reach overhead. This is important for dressing, getting things off shelves, or picking apples. You do not need to do all of these exercises. One exercise repeated three to ten times, two to four times a day, is sufficient. Pick the one that suits you best, or change exercises occasionally for variety.

12. The Shoulder Cradle

If your shoulder is still very painful, this exercise may be better tolerated. With your arm supported at the elbow by the opposite hand (A), raise the arm up over your head. You can rest your forearm on your head as you coax your shoulder just past the point of pain (B). This exercise may be easier lying down.

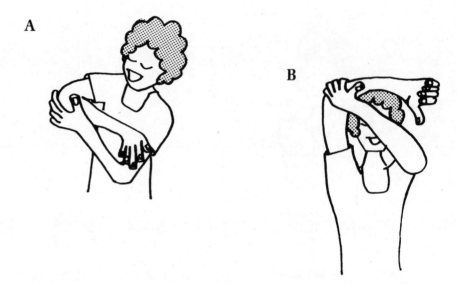

13. The Wand Exercise

Use a cane, yardstick, or mop handle as your wand. Place one hand on each end and raise the wand as high overhead as possible. You might try doing this in front of a mirror. You don't have to move both ends to the same height — play around with it. If holding the wand causes pain in your hand, try building up the grip area as described in Chapter 9. This exercise may be easier lying down or sitting.

14. The Shoulder Pulley

Throw a piece of rope over the top of an open door, creating a modified pulley system. Hold one end of the rope in each hand. As you pull down on one end, the other arm will be raised up. Coax the arm a little higher than it wants to go and then pull down, raising the opposite arm. This exercise can also be done while sitting.

HIPS

The hip is the largest joint of the body and like the shoulder can move in several directions. In choosing which exercise to do, decide which movements are most limited or painful and concentrate on them initially. You should do the selected exercises three to ten times, two to four times a day. Stretch just past the point of pain. If exercise-induced pain persists for longer than two hours after exercise, you are doing too much. *Do not stop,* just cut back.

15. The Spread Eagle

This exercise increases hip motion to the side, which is necessary for riding a bicycle, getting in and out of a car, or riding a horse. Lie on your back. Spread your legs as far apart as possible and then coax them a little farther. You might want someone to measure the distance between your knees so you can keep track of your progress. If this is difficult or if you feel discomfort in your lower back, move one leg at a time while keeping the other leg bent.

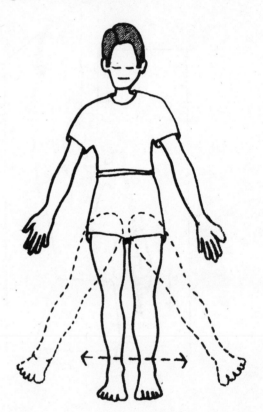

16. Knee-to-Chest

This exercise will help increase the hip motion forward, which is important for activities such as walking, climbing stairs, and getting on and off low furniture. Lie on your back. Keep one leg straight and bring your other knee toward your chest. You can place your hands under the thigh to assist with the stretch. This exercise also helps to stretch the low back. You may want to begin with your other leg slightly bent to decrease strain on the low back.

17. The Back Kick

This exercise is designed to increase the backward motion of the hip, which is important for walking, running, and cross-country skiing. From a standing position, hold on to a counter for support and move the leg up and back, knee straight. Start gently and keep your hips facing forward.

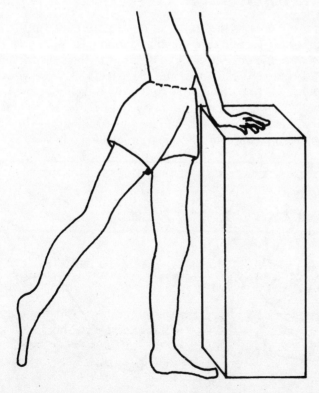

18. The Leg Lift

If you cannot stand up to do the Back Kick, this exercise also helps to increase the backward motion of the hip. Lie face down. This alone may provide a good stretch for those who spend a great deal of time sitting or in bed. If this position is comfortable, raise your leg as high as possible. This exercise should not be done by people with low back or disc problems.

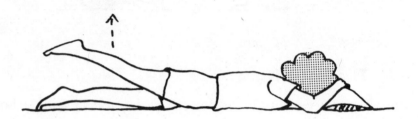

19. The Hip Rotator

This exercise increases the ability of the hip to rotate (roll in and out). This is important for activities such as dancing or rolling over and getting out of bed. Lie on your back, hands out to the side or behind your head. Bend your hips and knees and place feet flat. Cross your right leg over the left knee (A). Rotate hips to the right, trying to touch the knee to the floor (B). Keep your upper body flat on the floor. Repeat to the other side. This is also a good exercise for stretching the low and middle back, but some may find it too strenuous for the back.

A

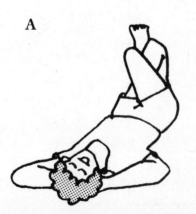

B

KNEES

The knee is subject to a lot of stress due to its weight-bearing duties and limited muscular support. When stretching the knee it is important to minimize the stress on the joint. Thus you should not be standing when you exercise your knees as the weight of your body adds stress.

The next two exercises are designed to increase your ability to bend and straighten the knee, which is important for climbing stairs or getting up and down from a chair, and most important for standing and walking without fatigue.

20. Knee Bend 1

Lie on your back with both knees bent, feet flat. Bring your knee toward your chest. Using your hands to assist, gently bend the knee, trying to touch your heel to your buttock.

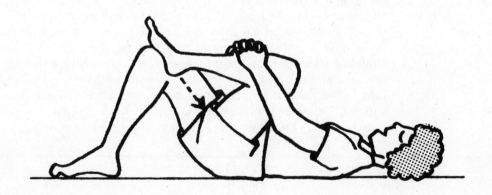

21. Knee Bend 2

If exercise 20 doesn't suit you, try this one. Sit on a straight-backed chair and bend your knee as far back as possible. (Be sure that it is not a part of the chair that keeps you from going farther.) To get an extra stretch, place your hands on the side of the chair and scoot forward toward the edge, keeping your feet in the same position.

22. The Knee Straightener

The ability to straighten the knee is very important for walking or any standing activity. When one spends a lot of time sitting, the muscles and ligaments in the back of the knee tend to tighten, making it difficult to completely straighten the knee. This exercise is designed to stretch these tissues with a minimum of stress on the joints. Sitting in a straight-backed chair, place your foot on a chair or high footstool. Bend the knee slightly and then straighten by pushing the back of the knee toward the floor. If you find this easy, add another stretch. Place the support. Carefully lean forward; keep your back straight. You will feel a stretch along the hamstring muscles on the back of your leg.

ANKLES AND FEET

23. The Achilles Stretch

This exercise is designed to stretch your Achilles tendon, which is the large tendon you feel at the back of your ankle. It is important to maintain flexibility in this tendon for standing and walking. Joggers should be sure to stretch this tendon before starting out. Doing this exercise before going to bed may help prevent leg cramps.

Stand at the end of a table and hold onto the sides. Bend the knee of the leg you are not stretching so it almost touches the table. Put the leg to be stretched behind you, keeping both feet flat on the floor. Now lean forward, keeping your back knee straight. You should feel a good stretch in the calf of the leg. This exercise can also be done leaning against a wall or fence.

24. The Heel-Toe

Sit in a chair or on the edge of the bed with both feet flat on the floor. First, raise your toes and forefeet as high as you can, keeping your heels on the floor (A). Then, keep your toes on the floor and raise your heels as high as you can (B). This stretches tendons, calf muscles, and the ankle joints.

A

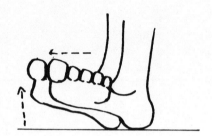

B

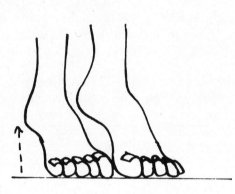

25. The Heel-Toe Dance

Sit in a chair with your feet flat on the ground. With heels on the floor, lift feet and toes as high as you can (A). Keeping the heels on the floor, move feet and toes to the right (B). Then come up on your toes as high as you can and move your heels to the right (C). Reverse and walk feet to the left in the same manner. This helps the rotation at the ankle.

A

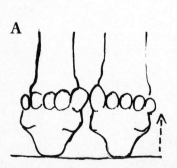

B

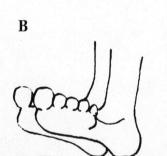

C

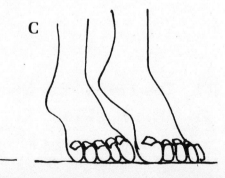

26. The Foot Roll

Place a dowel (large mop handle, closet rod, rolling pin) under the arch of the foot and roll it back and forth. This feels great and it stretches the ligaments of the arch of the foot.

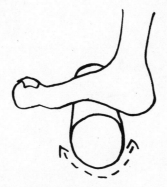

NECK

The neck involves many joints that work together to allow movement. It is one of the easiest parts of the body to exercise. However, it is important to be gentle when you exercise the neck. If you have learned to do neck exercises using circular motions, be sure you only make a half-circle in each direction. A complete circle may cause severe pain for people with bone spurs or a disc problem. If you have found circular exercises to be unsatisfactory, the following exercises should be more appropriate, and we prefer them.

If your neck pain is a new occurrence and the pain is moderate to severe, if you have pain that radiates down your arm with neck movement, or if numbness, tingling, or marked weakness are present in the arm, you should consult your physician or physical therapist before proceeding with these exercises.

27. The Three-Way Neck Stretch

1. Relax and slowly drop your chin to your chest, then slowly raise your head and very gently drop the head backward. Do not proceed with this exercise if you feel a sharp pain or pain down your arm.

Return head to the upright position slowly. This motion should never be forced.

2. Turn to look over your right shoulder, then turn to look as far over the left shoulder as possible.

3. Tilt your head to the right and then to the left. Try to touch your ear to your shoulder. If you find that this exercise makes you dizzy, try closing your eyes. If you are still dizzy, discontinue the exercise.

BACK

The following are a series of exercises for those with chronic back problems, especially those with ankylosing spondylitis or other forms of generalized stiffness. If your back pain is a new occurrence and the pain is moderate to severe, you should consult your physician or physical therapist before proceeding with these exercises. Also, if you notice pain that radiates down your leg, numbness, tingling, or marked weakness, consult a physician. If exercise-induced pain lasts longer than two hours, cut back a little. Those with ankylosing spondylitis will want to do deep-breathing exercises in addition to ensure good mobility of the rib cage.

28. The Pelvic Tilt

This exercise should be the beginning point for the person with low back problems. Lie on the bed or floor with both knees bent, feet flat. Place your hands on your abdomen. Flatten the small of your back against the floor by tightening your buttocks and pulling in your stomach. If this concept is difficult for you, think of bringing your pubic bone toward your chin. Once you have mastered the pelvic tilt in the lying position, try it while standing and sitting.

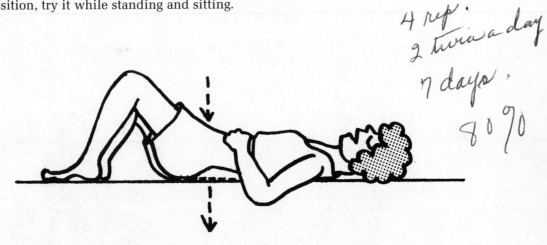

*4 rep.
2 twice a day
7 days.
8 0 90*

29. Knee-to-Chin Stretch

For a nice low back stretch, lie on the floor with knees bent, feet flat. Bring one knee toward your chin, using your hands to assist with the stretch. Maintain this position for five seconds and lower the leg slowly. Repeat with the other knee. To stretch the upper and middle back at the same time, raise your head and shoulder from the floor as you bring your knee toward your chin. If this creates or increases neck pain, discontinue this portion of the exercise.

30. The Low Back Rock

Lie on your back with your knees bent and feet flat. Pull knees up to chest, one at a time, grasping under the thighs to assist with the stretch. Rest in this position for five seconds, then gently rock knees from one side to the other, keeping upper back and shoulders on the floor.

31. The Shoulder-Blade Pinch

This is a good exercise for the middle and upper back. Sit on the edge of a bed or chair. Pinch your shoulder blades together by moving your elbows as far back as possible.

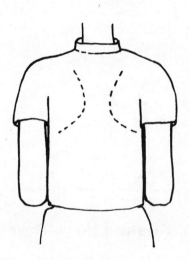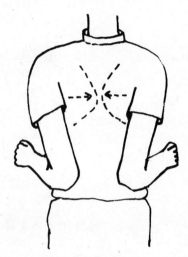

32. The Back Lift

Another way to improve flexibility of the spine is to lie on your stomach. Raise up onto your forearms. If you feel no discomfort, raise up onto extended arms. This exercise should be avoided by people with moderate to severe low back pain.

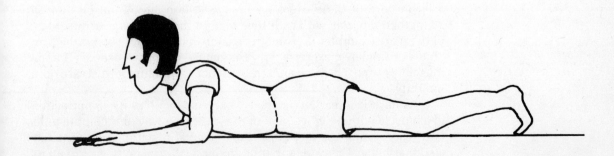

33. The Cat

This exercise should not be done by persons with severe knee, ankle, or hand problems because it places stress on these joints. Assume a crawling position on all fours, with knees bent, arms straight. Taking a deep breath, arch your back as a frightened cat does. Then slowly drop the arch, exhaling completely.

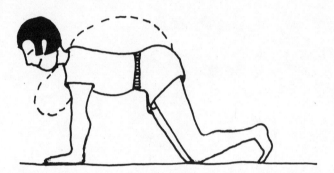

34. Stretch Like a Cat, Shake Like a Dog

This exercise, suggested by one of our friends with arthritis, not only gets you started in the morning but is also fun. Arthritis is a serious disease, but laughter helps. One of the common complaints of people who do not exercise is a lack of time. This exercise enables you to use your time efficiently by accomplishing two things at once. Since you spend a considerable amount of time in the bathroom every day, why not use that time to do a few exercises?

While sitting on the toilet: first stretch your arms and legs like a cat waking up, then pretend you are a dog just waking and shake all over.

STRENGTHENING EXERCISES

The purpose of these exercises is to maintain strong muscles and to strengthen muscles with as little stress on the joints as possible. Many of them are examples of isometric exercise. If you understand the principles of isometric exercise, you can devise your own exercise for any muscle group. These exercises will not maintain or increase joint mobility.

As described earlier, isometric exercise involves use (contraction) of a muscle with no movement of the joint. One way to accomplish this is to use the muscle to pull or push against a stationary object. The stationary object may be anything from a wall to a body part to an exercise belt. For example, place your hand on the wall and push. You can feel the muscles in your arm working; however, no movement of the joints is taking place. This is an isometric exercise. Here's another example: Sit in a chair and place your right hand on your right knee. Press your right knee against the hand, allowing no movement of the arm or leg. You have used another body part as the stationary object.

One nice thing about isometric exercises is that you do not have to do many to receive the benefits. **Each exercise,** held for a count of **six seconds, three to four times a day,** is sufficient. *Gradually* tense and relax the muscle, avoiding sudden, quick movement. To prevent the tendency to hold your breath, count the six seconds out loud. If exercise-induced pain lasts longer than two hours, cut back a little. As with the famous tortoise, slow and steady wins the race. Long, sustained isometric exercise is not advisable for heart patients, but the following exercises should not be harmful. If in doubt, consult your physician.

For these exercises you will need an exercise belt of some kind. It is best if this belt has some give to it. The inner tube from a bicycle tire, a bungie cord (holds packages on bicycles), or a strong stretch belt will do fine. If all else fails, a regular leather belt will suffice. The exercise belt is a closed loop, 30 to 48 inches in circumference.

Before proceeding to specific exercises, take a mental inventory of your body. Are there parts of your body you would like to strengthen? If so, define which parts.

1. _____ *back* _____ # 28 _____
2. _____ *shoulders* _____
3. _____ *knees* _____
4. _____ *ankles* _____
5. _____ *hips* _____

Now pick two or three priorities and proceed to the section dealing with your priority areas. Remember, your goal is not to do every strengthening exercise in the book but to use the ones you specifically need.

1. _____

2. _____

3. _____

HANDS

35. The Finger Press

To strengthen the muscles that bend the fingers and help you pick up objects, try this exercise. Lightly press the tip of the thumb to the tip of the index finger. Hold for six seconds, maintaining a perfect "O" shape, then relax. Continue, lightly pressing the tip of the thumb to the tip of each finger. To help maintain the "O" shape, place a pill bottle or other cylinder in your hand. Those with rheumatoid arthritis should not press the fingers together but just touch them lightly.

36. The Finger Lift

To strengthen the muscles that straighten the fingers, lay your hand flat on a table. Lay your other hand across the fingers to be exercised. Lift the fingers of the bottom hand, pushing against the top hand. Hold for six seconds; relax. If you have significant weakness, do each finger separately. You should exert only gentle pressure for this exercise.

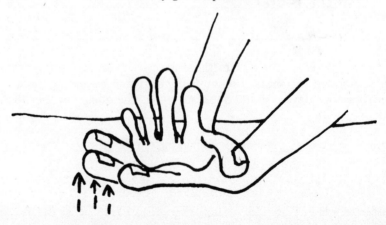

37. The Finger Slide

Place your hand flat, fingers spread, on the table. Lift and slide each finger toward the thumb. Resist slightly with the other hand. This will help prevent drifting of the fingers toward the little-finger side of the hand.

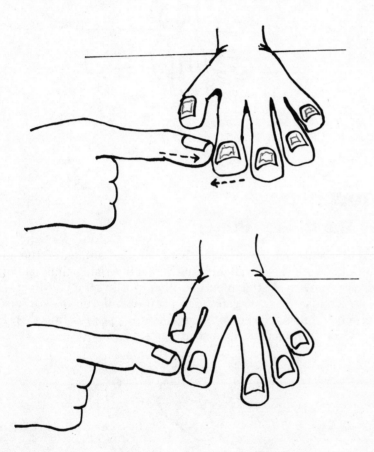

WRISTS

38. The Wrist Press

This exercise will strengthen the muscles that bend and straighten the wrist. Rest your hand on a table or armrest. Place the heel of the other hand on top. Raise the bottom hand, pushing against the top hand. Hold for six seconds, then relax. Reverse positions of the hand and repeat. Remember, while you are pressing the hands together, allow no joint movement. If it is painful to use your other hand as the stationary object, try to lift the hand against another stable object, such as the chair arm.

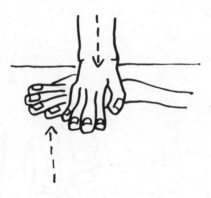

ELBOWS
39. The Biceps Bulge

This will strengthen the muscles that bend and straighten the elbow. Place your exercise belt slightly above each wrist, palms facing up. Bend one elbow and straighten the other, pulling the belt tight. Hold for six seconds. Relax. Reverse arm positions. If you do not have an exercise belt, cross your forearms, palms up, and press together. Hold for six seconds. Relax and reverse arm positions.

SHOULDERS
40. The Side Pull

Place the exercise belt around your forearms. With the elbows straight, palms facing each other, move your arms out to the side until the belt is tight. Hold for six seconds. Relax. If you do not have an exercise belt, perform the same movement, pushing against a wall, door frame, or some other stationary object.

41. The Robot

This exercise will strengthen the muscles that raise and lower your arm. Place the exercise belt around your forearms, palms down. Keeping elbows straight, pull up with one arm and down with the other until the belt is tight. Hold for six seconds, then relax. Reverse arm positions and repeat. If you do not have an exercise belt, perform the same movement using a table, wall, or your other forearm as the stationary object.

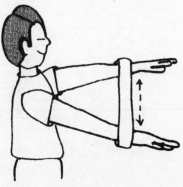

42. The Bow and Arrow

This is a fun exercise for strengthening many of the arm muscles. Hold the exercise belt in both hands. Push out to the side with one arm and pull back with the other, as if shooting a bow and arrow or a giant rubber band. Hold for six seconds, then relax. Reverse arm positions. Those with hand involvement should modify this exercise because gripping the belt causes stress. Be creative!

HIPS

43. The "Cheek to Cheek"

This exercise will strengthen the muscles that move your leg backward. Squeeze the buttocks tightly together. Hold for six seconds. Relax. This exercise may be done while lying down, sitting, or standing.

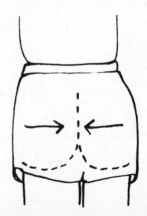

44. The Leg Spreader

The muscles that move your legs out to the side must be strong if you are to walk well. Lie on your back, with the exercise belt placed around your ankles. (If your knees are painful place the belt above the knees.) Spread your legs apart until the exercise belt is as tight as possible. Hold for six seconds, then relax. Do not let your foot roll in or out. You may do each leg separately if you wish.

45. The Straight-Leg Raise

This familiar old exercise will strengthen the muscles that bend the hip as well as the muscle that runs across the front of the knee. Lie on your back, arms in a comfortable position. Tighten the muscle that runs across the front of the knee and then raise your leg one to two feet off the ground, keeping the knee straight. Do not arch your back. Hold for six seconds. Relax. If you have low back discomfort you should do this exercise with the other knee bent. As your muscles become stronger, place the exercise belt around your ankles and perform the same exercise. Pull the belt tight, hold for six seconds, and then lower the leg slowly.

KNEES
46. The Quad Set

This is a good place for the person with very weak or painful knees to start. The exercise will strengthen the muscles that straighten the knee. These muscles are crucial for walking, going up and down stairs, or getting out of low furniture. Sit with your back supported, legs stretched out in front of you. (You may bend one knee if this is more comfortable.) Tighten the muscle that runs across the front of the knee by pulling your toes toward your head and pushing the back of the knee down into the bed or floor. Hold for six seconds. Relax. If sitting is difficult, this exercise may be done while lying down.

47. The Knee Scissor

Here's another exercise to strengthen the muscles that straighten the knee. It will also strengthen the muscles that bend the knee. Sit in a straight-backed chair. Place the exercise belt around both ankles. Straighten one knee while you pull back with the other until the belt is very tight. Hold for six seconds. Relax. To reduce stress on the knee joint, lean back slightly as you do this exercise.

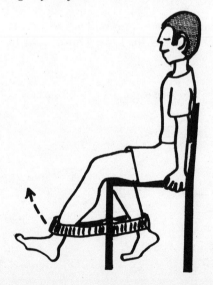

48. The Heel Press

To strengthen the muscles at the back of the thigh that bend the knee, sit in a straight-backed chair. Bend the knee, pressing the heel against the leg of the chair. Hold for six seconds. Relax.

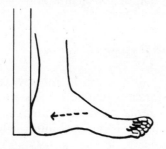

ANKLES AND FEET

49. The Tiptoe

Holding on lightly to a counter or table for support, raise up on your tiptoes (A). Hold for six seconds. Lower slowly. This exercise may be too stressful for some, especially if you are overweight. As an alternative exercise, place the sole of your foot against a stationary object (wall, chair leg) and push (B). Hold for six seconds; relax.

A

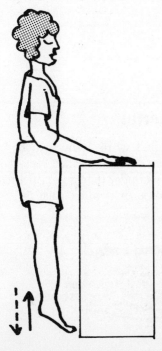

B

NECK

If your neck pain is a new occurrence and the pain is moderate to severe, if you have pain that radiates down your arm with neck movement, or if numbness, tingling, or marked weakness are present in the arm, consult a physician or physical therapist before proceeding with these exercises.

50. The Head Press

Here is an easy way to strengthen the muscles that bend and straighten the neck. Place your forearm against your forehead and press with your head. Hold for six seconds, allowing no movement. Relax. Then place your forearm on the back of the head and push. Hold for six seconds. Relax. If you cannot use your arm as the stationary object, a wall or a car headrest will do just as well.

51. The Neck Strengthener

The same muscles can be strengthened while lying in bed. Lift your head up off the pillow. Hold for six seconds, then relax. Press your head down into the pillow. Hold for six seconds, then relax. If lifting your head is painful, press against your forearm as in exercise 50.

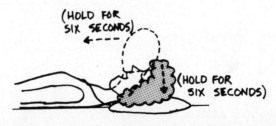

BACK AND STOMACH

If your back pain is a new occurrence and the pain is moderate to severe, if pain radiates down your leg or around to the chest, or if numbness, tingling, or marked weakness exist, consult a physician or physical therapist before proceeding.

Firm stomach and back muscles are important to provide the support necessary for an erect posture and to avoid back strain. In addition to the following exercises, the Pelvic Tilt (exercise 28) is helpful and should be done frequently during the day, in any position.

52. The Partial Sit-Up

It is not necessary to do a full sit-up to exercise the stomach muscles. A partial sit-up will place less stress on the joints and is sufficient. Lie on your back on a firm surface, knees bent, feet flat. Raise your head and shoulders as far off the surface as possible. Hold for six seconds, then lower slowly. Breathe out as you raise your body, count to six out loud as you hold, and breathe in as you lower your body. *Do not hold your breath.* If your neck is painful during this exercise, try the next one instead. Don't cheat by tucking your feet under a chair!

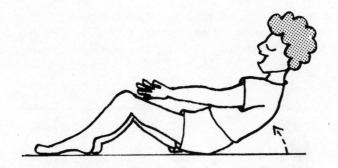

53. The Back Sit

This is a fun alternative to the sit-up and is easier on the neck. Sit upright on a firm surface. Lean partially backward, hold for six seconds, then return to sitting. As your stomach muscles strengthen you should be able to lean farther and farther backward. Breathe out as you lean back, count to six out loud as you hold, and breathe in as you return to sitting.

54. The Back Push

To strengthen the muscles that straighten the back, sit in a straight-backed chair or against the wall. Push your shoulders and shoulder blades into the chair or wall. Hold for six seconds. Relax. You will feel the stomach muscles tighten as well; the stomach muscles help support the back.

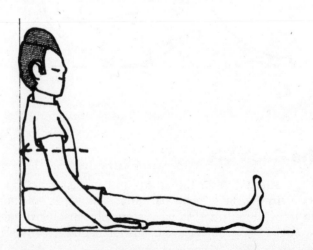

55. The Back Lift

This exercise will also strengthen the muscles that straighten the back, but it is more strenuous. Lie on your stomach, arms at your sides. Lift your head, shoulders, and arms up off the floor or bed. Hold for six seconds. Relax. If this does not feel too stressful, try lifting your legs off the floor at the same time. This is generally not a good exercise for the person with moderate to severe low back pain but is beneficial for the person with general stiffness or ankylosing spondylitis.

JAWS

56. The Jaw Loosener

Problems at the temporomandibular joint (TMJ), or jaw, can be caused or worsened by clenching and grinding your teeth. This exercise will teach you to keep the teeth apart.

Let the lower jaw hang slack so that none of the teeth touch and an opening of a quarter of an inch, or approximately the thickness of a thumb, exists between the teeth. Practice this exercise five times a day or more for at least thirty seconds.

The jaw loosener may be done with the lips together or apart. Some people find they are better able to relax their muscles by thinking about relaxing.

It helps to repeat silently a phrase, such as "lips together, teeth apart," or "let jaw hang," while practicing. Try to pair this exercise with an activity you find yourself doing frequently throughout the day, for example, getting in or out of your car or hanging up the phone, so that each time you do the activity you will be reminded to practice the exercise.

The only time the teeth should touch is during swallowing and chewing. Avoid habits that overuse the jaw muscles and joints, such as gum chewing, pencil and nail biting, leaning chin on hands, and smoking. Also, avoid foods which require prolonged chewing, such as tough meats and hard bread crusts. Be aware of your jaw position in doing any activity that involves resistance (weightlifting, moving furniture, nail clipping, cutting or slicing tough foods), because of the strong, instinctive tendency to clench your teeth during these activities.

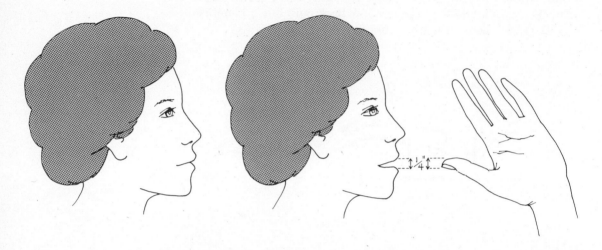

ENDURANCE EXERCISE

In the last few years, endurance, or aerobic, exercise has become very popular. Not everyone with arthritis can run, bicycle, swim, or walk several blocks. However, most everyone can do some endurance exercise.

An endurance exercise can be any activity that causes you to breathe a little harder and raises your heart rate. To get the full benefit of endurance exercise, you need to exercise for about 20 minutes at least three times a week, but if you are just beginning to exercise, it's best to start with shorter exercise periods and increase gradually.

Checking with Your Doctor

Before starting an endurance exercise program, it is best to check with your physician. You might even take this book with you to let your doctor know what kind of exercises you are thinking of. Review your exercise strategy with your doctor, telling him or her how many and what kinds of strengthening and range of motion exercises you are going to combine with endurance activities and at what rate you will increase them.

Choosing an Exercise

This is not as easy as it sounds. There are many types of exercises that are excellent. Walking, swimming, and bicycling are three of the most common endurance exercises. Other people play tennis, folk dance, or climb stairs. Activities such as gardening and house cleaning usually don't qualify as endurance exercises; however, mowing the lawn will give you a good workout.

Choose one or two exercises that you enjoy (or least like) and that don't put undue stress on your joints. For example, even if you have arthritis in your knees, you can do some walking or bicycling, but you should start slowly and build up slowly. The exercises should be something that you can easily work into your daily routine. If the exercise is something new to you, try it out before committing yourself to what could be an expensive venture. For example, borrow a friend's exercise bike or try using one in the exercise room of your community college. Many health clubs have exercise bikes they might be willing to let you try.

If swimming is what you want to do, look for a recreational pool in your area. Many hotels and motels sell memberships to use their pools, or possibly, you could make a private arrangement. Many apartment complexes have pools. Check to see if you can become a "permanent guest of friend." YMCAs and YWCAs often have pools; some are even special warm, winter pools. In some locations the Arthritis Foundation offers water exercise programs.

Developing a Program

Start Where You Are

One of the biggest problems with endurance exercise is overdoing it at first. When one overdoes, the results are exhaustion and sore muscles and joints. Remember the Two-Hour Pain Rule: if your exercise causes pain that continues two hours after exercising, cut back. Extended pain will lead to a growing dislike of exercise. To avoid this, think about what you can comfortably do now. This may be to walk one or two blocks or to ride an exercise bicycle for one minute. Don't be worried if you can't do very much; this will change. The important thing is to start doing what you can now even if this is only walking across the room. As one woman told us, "When I started walking ten months ago, I walked two blocks a day. Now, I can walk a mile easily and really enjoy it." Build up your exercise program *slowly*.

There are three ways to add to your exercise program: adding distance, adding time, and carrying additional weights. The rule is never add more than one of these at a time and then just a little bit.

Distance

If you can now easily walk two blocks, you should do this at least three times a week for ten days to two weeks and then add a half a block to a block. Again, keep this schedule for another ten days to two weeks and again add half a block. Continue doing this until you are walking six to twelve blocks at least three times a week. Of course, if you are comfortable and having no problems, walking a mile or more a day is great exercise.

This same principle holds true with swimming and stair climbing. Do what you can do comfortably for ten days to two weeks, then add a little. Resist the temptation to progress too quickly. As you add distance, you will probably be adding time. Thus, time and distance often go together.

Time

A second way to increase endurance exercise is to add time. You may start out exercising only three to five minutes. This is fine. Again, do whatever is comfortable. After a week or so, add a few minutes (less than five) to your regime and continue doing so until you are exercising twenty to twenty-five minutes every day. Another way to use time is to remember the principles of mixing activity with rest. If you find sustained activity is tiring, try exercising (walking, climbing steps, bicycling) for three to four minutes and then rest for a minute or a minute and a half. Repeat the whole cycle. You might start with just two rest/exercise cycles and slowly build (one cycle every ten days) working up to five cycles. Be careful not to rest too much. The program should look something like this:

exercise	rest	exercise	rest	exercise
3 minutes	1 minute	3 minutes	1 minute	3 minutes

You don't *have* to break your exercise period with short rests, but you can if you find this easier.

Weight

By adding weight we don't mean body weight!! However, you can increase your endurance exercise, especially if you are walking or climbing stairs, by carrying a small weight in each hand. Here are some ideas of things to carry. Start out with something light, maybe a small stone. Some folks like to carry a lemon in each hand. It may look a little strange, but you can tell your friends that you are "walking your lemon." If you find that you like increasing your exercise program by adding weight, work yourself up to carrying a soup can in each hand.

Again, the rule is to only add a few ounces at a time and not more often than every ten days to two weeks.

A word of caution: if you have problems with your hands, wrists, elbows, or shoulders, carrying extra weight may put extra stress on the joints. In such circumstances, it is best to forget about using weights or use them with extreme caution.

For those of you who are swimmers, the principle of adding weight can be accomplished by wearing two bathing suits. The extra suit adds to your drag through the water. If you don't want to wear an extra suit, you can wear a T-shirt and your regular suit (applies to men and women).

WALKING

Walking is probably the most common form of exercise. In fact, it's so common, many people don't think of it as exercise. Walking has many of the benefits of jogging without the strain to our body. If you walk briskly, and swing your arms, you'll be getting practically all the benefits of jogging without the strain on your body.

Even at a slow pace walking is good for the leg and hip muscles. It can be a great exercise for the heart, lungs, and arms as well. Walking also helps to prevent and slow osteoporosis. Whether you are strolling along a pretty street or briskly marching off to the supermarket, walking is good exercise. Whatever your level of fitness, you are in condition to start a walking program.

Remember to follow the guidelines about increasing your walking. Add time, distance, or weight using a moderate schedule and your common sense. As you become more comfortable with your walking schedule and want to increase your fitness level, here are some suggestions.

1. **Use your arms.** Swing your arms when you walk. This will allow you to exercise most of the major muscles in the body, along with the heart and lungs. Remember to start with smaller arm swings and build up to shoulder height (similar to British soldiers marching). If you are having any sort of trouble in your shoulder or neck, approach the arm swinging cautiously. When swinging your arms, try to keep your arms and legs in some rhythm; you may have to slow your walking pace until your arms are up to beat. If you add a little weight (lemons, stones), your arm swinging will tone muscles and give your heart and lungs a real workout.

2. **Intervals.** The exercise-rest-exercise principle works well with walking. For example, one way to do this is to walk briskly for three

minutes and then slow to a more leisurely pace for one minute. Repeat this sequence for up to twenty-five minutes.

3. **Breathing.** Breathe deeply in rhythm with your walking pace. For example, inhale for three steps and exhale for three steps while keeping the lips slightly pursed. Keep the time of the inhale and the exhale the same. Slowly increase the time for each breath as your stamina improves. This is a great exercise for the lungs.

Advantages	Disadvantages
easy: almost anyone can walk	bad weather can be a problem
convenient	hard for people with bad feet, knees, or hips
excellent for health	

OVERCOMING OBSTACLES

1. **"Where we live, we don't have blocks." "I can't even walk a block."**   If one or both of these above problems applies to you, don't worry, they have simple solutions. If you don't have blocks or can't walk that far yet, count driveways or trees or telephone poles. Choose guideposts that measure distances you can be comfortable with and add slowly. As you progress, you may want to change guideposts.

2. **"Where I live, it rains (snows, sleets, is 120° . . .) for several months a year."**   It is certainly true that the weather doesn't always cooperate with an exercise program. With a little imagination, most people can find a way to exercise indoors. For example, shopping malls are wonderful for long walks. Just take a turn, or 10 turns, around the mall. You might even call a friend to walk with you and then have lunch or do some shopping. Supermarkets aren't quite as good and it may be hard to resist all the tempting foods. However, in a pinch, several trips up and down all the aisles is better than nothing. Also, on days when you can't go outdoors, you might try some alternative activity such as using a stationary bicycle or climbing steps.

3. **"I'm afraid I'll get too tired and won't be able to get back."**   Remember that you can walk a mile without ever leaving your own block. Walk up one side and down the other. In a standard block, doing this five times is equivalent to walking a mile and you are never more than a block from home.

SWIMMING AND AQUATIC EXERCISES

Swimming is another very good exercise for people with arthritis. The buoyancy of the water allows you to move your joints through the full range of motion without the stress of loading that even standing may put on your hips, knees, and feet.

If you haven't been swimming for a while, it might be useful to take a refresher course at the local Y. To receive the full aerobic benefits of swimming, you need to swim laps or exercise in the shallow end.

The shallow end of the pool is a great place to do your stretching or range-of-motion exercises. The buoyancy and the resistance of the water forces you to work harder while you are being supported by the water. Aquatic exercise classes are becoming popular; contact your nearest Arthritis Foundation. These are similar to the popular dance/exercise classes but much safer for someone with arthritis.

Here are a few pointers to make the most out of water exercise:

- Join a class to add excitement and social support.

- If you're rusty, a little coaching can help a lot.

- Swim at your own pace, relax; it will be much easier.

- Find a heated pool (the Arthritis Foundation recommends 80 to 84°).

Advantages	Disadvantages
less strain on joints	may be hard to find a pool
great for range-of-motion exercises	you may not be able to swim
	cold weather could be a problem

BICYCLING

Bicycling is a pleasant way to get in shape and it is a great way to get to the supermarket or do some local shopping. Bicycling can be a lot of fun if done safely. It's even more fun with family or friends.

If you haven't been on a bicycle for a long time, be careful until your sense of balance improves. If you don't feel up to relearning how to ride a bicycle, you might try a three-wheeler. The three-wheel design makes it almost impossible to fall and very good for carrying groceries.

An indoor stationary bicycle is another way to avoid problems with balance and falling.

Bicycle safety is very important. Observe the rules of the road and ride defensively when in traffic. Many people simply avoid busy streets with traffic and ride on the quiet, little-traveled streets; it's much safer and often more pleasant. Safety equipment such as reflectors and a lightweight helmet are a must. Your bicycle dealer can advise about the equipment available.

If you have decided to buy a bicycle, it's wise to ask the dealer for help in choosing the right one. Your height and leg and arm length are all factors when choosing a bicycle. The wrong-sized bicycle may end up aggravating your aches and pains. Also, many people find that the down-turned handlebars commonly found on the ten-speed bicycles are uncomfortable and cause shoulder and back strain. You do not need an expensive bicycle with 10 or 15 gears to get the health benefits and pleasure of bicycling — you may even be able to buy a used bicycle with fewer gears for less than $50. If you have knee problems, be sure to ride in a comfortable gear.

Here are some pointers for bicyclists:

- Know and observe the rules of the road; ride defensively.

- Use the proper safety equipment including a helmet.

- Avoid heavy automobile traffic.

- Find pleasant areas with natural scenery.

- Try it with friends.

Advantages	Disadvantages
you can save on gas	traffic can be hazardous
you can bicycle with friends	bad weather may dampen your enthusiasm
the scenery is always changing	bicycles can be expensive

STATIONARY BICYCLES

These offer all the benefits of bicycling without the hazards of traffic, bad weather, and barking dogs. Instead of snacking and watching your favorite soap opera, you can bike your way to health without missing a single commercial.

Stationary bicycles come in many models, from the very simple to quite sophisticated. With each added feature, the cost of the bicycle goes up, and while none of them are necessary, they can be beneficial. Most have a speedometer and odometer to let you know your speed and the "distance" you traveled. Often, the stationary bikes have a lever or knob to set the "resistance" and make it easier or harder to pedal. Make sure you start at a low level and change the resistance only after you have exercised for two weeks at the lower level. Raising resistance when biking is like adding weights when walking. Another feature commonly found on stationary bicycles are handlebars that can be pushed forward and back to simulate a rowing motion. This means that while you are pedaling, you can also exercise your arms, shoulders, and back. This is a very complete exercise but needs to be approached cautiously. The rowing motion may aggravate the back or arthritis in the hands and shoulders. As with all exercises, build up slowly.

Before you buy a stationary bicycle, try one and see how it feels. As with regular bicycles, the correct size is important; the wrong size can be quite uncomfortable. Sometimes the dealer will let you take one home on a trial basis or you can rent one from a medical supply house. Shop around and ask several dealers for advice.

Tips for using a stationary bicycle:

- Start slowly.

- Move to the next resistance level after you have been at your present level for two weeks.

Advantages	Disadvantages
convenience; it's always available and you can listen to music or watch TV or chat with a friend	some people find it boring (unless there is something to distract you)
it's very safe if you are careful stepping on and off	added expense; but you could consider it an investment for your health
privacy	takes up room in your house
consistent; weather or traffic, etc., will not interrupt your exercise	

STAIR CLIMBING

This is a very inexpensive, indoor exercise that can be very beneficial for the heart, lungs, and leg muscles. If you have problems with your knees and hips, this exercise isn't advisable; walking is more appropriate. Start slowly — climbing uphill or upstairs increases the workload and you can raise your heart rate while going quite slowly. Because stair climbing can be strenuous, pause periodically and see how you are feeling. Intervals work well with stair climbing. Climb up and down the stairs for one minute, rest for one minute, and repeat this cycle for ten minutes. If at first this is too much, don't worry. Do as much as you can and slowly increase the time up to twenty-five minutes.

Pointers for stair climbing:

- Keep your back straight.

- Use a railing.

- Try it with music.

Advantages	**Disadvantages**
efficient exercise	could become boring
private, convenient	
inexpensive	

A MATTER OF PRINCIPLE: EXERCISE REVIEW

Let's go back over the critical points. The three important kinds of exercise to maintain and improve the function of arthritic joints and surrounding muscles are:

1. **Stretching exercises** to maintain and increase joint mobility and thus function. They should be performed three to ten times a session, two to four times a day, depending on pain.

2. **Strengthening exercises** to increase muscle strength and improve the ability to bear weight, lift objects, and sustain movement. Usually, isometric exercises are best. Hold each exercise for six seconds and repeat three to four times once a day.

3. **Endurance exercise** to increase your endurance, maintain a strong heart and bones, and reduce fatigue. The goal is to do some sort of endurance exercise for twenty minutes three to four times a week.

Balance your exercise activities with times of rest during the day. You can combine rest periods with relaxation training. Also remember that it is important to prepare for exercise by warming up.

Design your own exercise program to meet your special needs. Assess each exercise for its benefit to your priority joints and for any excessive stress on other involved joints. Begin slowly and build your program according to your response to the exercise. If at any time exercise-induced pain continues for more than two hours after exercise, you are doing too much. Do not stop exercising, but cut back a little. Remember, if you have a hot joint, restrain yourself to moving the joint through its full range of motion twice a day.

A MATTER OF PROGRAM: SETTING UP YOUR OWN EXERCISE PROGRAM

Now that you have chosen specific exercises, it may be helpful to write out your exercise program and keep an exercise diary. This tends to help you get started, and when you look back on it, it will show you how far you have progressed.

GUIDELINES

The following will give you some guidelines for setting up your exercise program. Read these guidelines carefully and use them as you plan your program.

Stretching Exercises (Exercises 1–34)

1. Start doing three repetitions of each exercise twice a day.

2. If for four days you have no exercise-induced pain lasting longer than two hours, add two repetitions (five in all) and do the exercises three times a day.

3. If no exercise-induced pain lasting longer than two hours is present in an additional four-day period, add two more repetitions (seven in all) and do the exercises four times a day.

4. If in the next four days you have no exercise-induced pain lasting longer than two hours, add three more repetitions (ten in all) and do the exercises four times a day.

5. If exercise-induced pain continues for more than two hours after exercise, cut back to the next lowest level and continue at that level for four days, then try the next highest level again.

6. If exercise-induced pain lasting longer than two hours occurs at the first level, try not to stretch so far (just past the point of pain). If pain still persists, cut back to two repetitions once a day or choose a different exercise that will achieve the same result.

7. Once you have reached your goal for a joint, remember to move it through its maximal range at least once or twice a day. This will ensure that you maintain the mobility that you worked so hard to obtain. If you notice that you are losing ground with that joint, then resume a more concentrated exercise program.

Strengthening Exercises (Exercises 35–56)

1. Start doing each exercise twice, once a day.

2. If no exercise-induced pain lasting longer than two hours occurs in a four-day period, add one repetition (three in all).

3. If no exercise-induced pain occurs for four more days, add one repetition (four in all).

4. If exercise-induced pain continues for more than two hours after exercise, cut back to the next lowest level and continue at that level for four days, then try to move to the next highest level again.

5. If pain occurs at the first level, reduce the force of your exercise. If pain still persists, cut back to doing the exercise only once.

Endurance Exercise

1. Choose one or more activity (walking, swimming, bicycling).

2. Determine how much you can comfortably do now.

3. Do this activity three to four times a week.

4. After ten days add about one-fourth more activity. For example, if you are walking four blocks, start walking five.

5. Every week to ten days add to your endurance exercise program until you are walking one mile or exercising twenty to thirty minutes, four times a week.

KEEPING AN EXERCISE DIARY

If you keep a record of your exercise, you can track your progress. When starting an exercise program, it is especially important to keep a daily diary until the habit is firmly established. This should take five to six weeks. Here are two hints for a successful program:

1. Put your diary where you will see it. Good places are your bathroom mirror or refrigerator.

2. Fill your diary out *every* day.

EXERCISE DIARY Week 1

Day	Name or Number of Exercise	How Much or Number of Repetitions	How Many Times a Day

Monday
  Stretching
  Strengthening
  Endurance			

Tuesday
  Stretching
  Strengthening
  Endurance			

Wednesday
  Stretching
  Strengthening
  Endurance			

Thursday
  Stretching
  Strengthening
  Endurance			

Friday
  Stretching
  Strengthening
  Endurance			

Saturday
  Stretching
  Strengthening
  Endurance			

Sunday
  Stretching
  Strengthening
  Endurance			

WHY I DON'T EXERCISE

If you've read this far and you still have reservations about exercising, this section is for you.

You now know all the advantages of exercise and how to choose an appropriate program for your needs. Still many of you are not exercising. Let's explore some of the common complaints about exercise and some hints on how to get around them.

1. **"I don't have enough time to exercise. Exercise will make me tired."** As it happens, regular exercisers find that they feel more energetic and efficient. Rather than being another burden, exercise can help you get through your schedule more efficiently. Try this: For two weeks, set up an exercise schedule that includes exercise at least every other day. Stick to it! You'll probably find that there's not enough time *not* to exercise.

2. **"I'm too embarrassed to exercise."** If you feel self-conscious about exercising in public, you've got lots of company. You might be embarrassed because you don't know how to do a certain exercise. Just remember that everyone started out where you are and you'll get the hang of it. It's more important to get started doing something you enjoy doing; improvement will come naturally. If you're embarrassed about your appearance, look around at the people you see jogging or in swimming pools. Nowadays, people of all shapes and sizes are exercising to improve their health. With exercise, you really do get an "A" for effort, not for how you look.

3. **"I hate exercise."** Today it is not fashionable to say this, but for many of us, it is true. There is nothing we can say to make you like exercise, but we can guarantee you that if you embark on an exercise program that is comfortable for you, it will give you a new, better outlook. We urge you to at least try exercising; you may be surprised at how good you can feel. Here are some suggestions to make exercising a little easier:

   a. Try to figure out what you don't like and correct the problems. If you don't like to sweat, remember that you don't have to sweat when walking; or, try swimming. Try exercising early in the morning or in the evening when it is cooler.

   b. If you like the idea of water exercise but can't swim, take swimming lessons or just walk in the water. Walking in water is great exercise as the water gives resistance while lessening strain on the joints.

c. If exercise bores you, do something different each time: walking, stair climbing, or try listening to music or talk shows as you exercise.

d. Exercise while watching TV or listening to the radio.

e. Exercising with a friend will make it less of a chore. Any exercise, except swimming, can be done while catching up on the latest news with a friend. In fact, if you are too short of breath to talk while exercising, you are working too hard and should slow down. If you are bored with exercise, take a friend along and share both the boredom and the benefits of exercise.

f. Make a small commitment that isn't too demanding. You do not need to start out with a full-blown exercise regimen. Rather, start slowly and ease into a daily routine.

g. Reward yourself. Put off some favorite activity until after you've exercised. For example, make an agreement with yourself not to read the morning paper until you're through exercising.

h. Don't underrate taking a short walk after dinner or doing a few strengthening exercises while waiting for a light to change.

The purpose of exercise is to help you:

1. Regain coordination and *strength*.

2. Increase your *endurance*.

3. Prevent and decrease deformity (usually through *stretching*).

4. Increase your *functional ability*.

8

Pain Management

Pain is a problem shared by most people with arthritis. In fact, for many people, it is their number-one concern. Unfortunately, pain is a very personal symptom. It cannot be seen by others and we do not even have good words to describe most pain. Because pain is so important, most arthritis treatment is aimed, in part, at pain relief. Thus, the use of heat, medications, exercise, and even cold can all help reduce pain. There are also a whole set of nondrug pain-management techniques that are seldom taught. Like all activities, they require some skill, but their mastery has brought relief to many people. In the following pages, we describe several pain-management techniques.

To use these techniques to the best advantage we suggest that:

1. You read the whole chapter.

2. Try several different techniques. You will probably like some and not like others as well.

3. Try a specific technique at least twice a day for two weeks to find out if it will be helpful to you.

4. Once you have found two or three techniques you like, think how you will use each one. For example, some exercises can be done anywhere, while others require a quiet place. The best pain managers use a variety of techniques that can be mixed and matched to the situations in daily life.

5. Finally, place some cues in your environment to remind you to practice your pain-management skills. You have to be regular with your pain-management program for it to work. For example, place stars or other stickers where you will see them and they will remind you to practice your skills. You can put a star on your mirror, office or home telephone, or car dashboard. Change the stickers every month or so. This will help you "see" them.

RELAXATION TECHNIQUES

So much has been said and written about relaxation that most of us are completely confused. It is not a cure-all, but neither is it a hoax. Rather, like most treatment methods, it has specific uses in the management of arthritis. The advantage of relaxation is that your muscles become less tense and thus it is easier and less painful to move the joints. In addition to the release of residual tension throughout the body, these techniques are useful in helping you sleep. Relaxation exercises seem to be particularly helpful in relieving pain.

Like exercise, the following techniques take practice. Thus, if you do not feel you are accomplishing anything, be patient and keep trying. Feel free to try another method if the one you have chosen does not seem to work for you, but give it two full weeks trial. Relaxation techniques should be practiced at least twice a day. With many forms of arthritis, it is wise to take short rest periods during the day to avoid undue fatigue and to relieve stress on the joints. This is an excellent time to practice relaxation techniques.

The following are examples of relaxation techniques. Once you choose the one that works best for you, it may be helpful to tape record the technique. This is not necessary but is sometimes helpful if you find it hard to concentrate or follow the routine. With an inexpensive cassette recorder, you can make a tape to follow so that you don't have to think hard or look at this book while you are trying to relax.

Here are some guidelines that will help you practice the relaxation techniques described in this chapter:

1. Pick a quiet time and place where you will not be disturbed for fifteen to twenty minutes.

2. Try to practice twice daily, but not less than four times a week.

3. Don't expect miracles. It will probably take three to four weeks of practice before you really start to notice benefits.

4. Relaxation should be helpful. At worst, you may find it boring, but if it is unpleasant or makes you nervous, then you might do better with other pain-management techniques.

JACOBSON PROGRESSIVE RELAXATION

Many years ago, a psychiatrist, Edmund Jacobson, discovered that if a person wants to relax he or she must learn what it feels like to be relaxed and to be tense. Thus, he designed a very simple set of exercises to assist with the learning process. Jacobson felt that if one could recognize tension he or she could then let it go and relax. Progressive relaxation is best done lying on your back either on a rug or in bed. However, it can be done seated in a comfortable chair. Choose a quiet time and place where you will not be disturbed for at least fifteen minutes.

Technique for Progressive Relaxation of Each Muscle Group

First, for each muscle group of the arms and shoulders:

- Tense (contract) the muscles, holding until the tension is located (two to five seconds).

- Feel the tension, notice it carefully.
  Now release, let the tension slide away, all away.

- Feel the difference.

- Notice the pleasant warmth of relaxation.

- Repeat this sequence with the same group, but use only about half the tension.

- Repeat again with the same muscle group, but allow little movement so that only slight tension can be detected.

For the muscle groups of the lower limbs, trunk, and face it is only necessary to tense the muscle once, very slightly — just enough to recognize the tension. Then let it slide away. Feel the difference. Notice the pleasant warmth of relaxation.

MUSCLE GROUPS	TENSION EXERCISES
1. Dominant hand	Lift hand and make a fist; relax.
Other hand	Lift hand and make a fist; relax.
2. Dominant arm	Lift arm at shoulder; relax.
Other arm	Lift arm at shoulder; relax.
3. Shoulders	Shrug shoulders; relax.

Repeat each of the above three times with progressively less tension.

MUSCLE GROUPS	TENSION EXERCISES
4. Right foot	Bend toes, relax; lift toes, relax.
Left foot	Bend toes, relax; lift toes, relax.
5. Right leg	Start to bend knee (drag heel up slightly); relax.
Left leg	Start to bend knee (drag heel up slightly); relax.
6. Buttocks	Squeeze together; relax.
7. Abdomen	Make abdomen tight and hard; relax.
8. Chest and neck	Squeeze shoulder blades together and slightly arch back, pressing head backward; relax.
9. Breathing	Take a slow deep breath and relax completely as you exhale. Repeat two or three times.
10. Upper face and scalp	Raise eyebrows; relax. Close eyes tightly; relax.
11. Center face	Scowl and wrinkle nose; relax. Widen cheeks and brow; relax.
12. Lower face	Purse lips; relax. Smile; relax. Drop jaw; relax.
13. Breathing	Take a slow deep breath and relax completely as you exhale. Repeat two or three times.

Technique for Progressive Relaxation of the Whole Body*

- Tense all the muscles together and hold for five seconds.

- Feel the tension, notice it carefully, then release. Let all the tension slide away.

- Notice any remaining tension. Release it.

- Take a deep breath. Say "relax" softly to yourself as you breathe out slowly. Imagine the word *relax* written in warm sand.

- Remain totally relaxed.

- Repeat breathing in and out slowly, saying "relax," staying perfectly relaxed.

- Do this three times.

- The exercise has ended — enjoy the relaxation.

Jacobson emphasizes that the only purpose of voluntarily tensing the muscles is to learn to recognize and locate the tension in your body. Hopefully, you will then become aware of the minor states of involuntary tension and use the same procedure of letting go. Once learned it is unnecessary to tense voluntarily, just locate the tension and let it go.

For people with very painful joints, the Jacobson technique may not be the best exercise for relaxation. If it causes any pain, the pain may distract from the relaxation. If this is the case for you, try the following techniques.

THE RELAXATION RESPONSE

During the early 1970s, Dr. Herbert Benson did extensive work on what he calls the relaxation response. He says that our bodies have several natural states. For example, if you meet a lion on the street, you will probably become quite tense. In fact, the response will be a "fight or flight" response. After extreme tension, the body's natural response is to relax. This is what happens after a sexual climax. As life has become more and more complex, our bodies tend to stay in a constant state of tension. Thus, to elicit the relaxation response, many people need to consciously practice the following exercise.

---

*   Much of this section has been adapted from Gordon Paul. *Insight vs. Desensitization in Psychotherapy: An Experiment in Anxiety Reduction* (Stanford, Calif.: Stanford University Press, 1966).

Four Basic Elements

1. **A quiet environment.** "Turn off" not only internal stimuli but also distractions.

2. **An object to dwell upon or a mental device,** for example, repeating a word or sound like the word *one*, gazing at a symbol like a flower, or concentrating on a feeling, such as peace.

3. **A passive attitude.** This is the most essential factor. It is an emptying of all thoughts and distractions from your mind. Thoughts, imagery, and feeling may drift into awareness — don't concentrate on them, but allow them to pass on.

4. **A comfortable position.** You should be comfortable enough to remain in the same position for 20 minutes.

Technique for Eliciting the Relaxation Response

1. Sit quietly in a comfortable position.

2. Close your eyes.

3. Deeply relax all your muscles, beginning at your feet and progressing up to your face. Keep them relaxed.

4. Breathe in through your nose. Become aware of your breathing. As you breathe out through your mouth, say the word *one* silently to yourself. Try to empty all thoughts from your mind, concentrate on one.

5. Continue for 10 to 20 minutes — you may open your eyes to check the time, but do not use an alarm. When you finish, sit quietly for several minutes, at first with your eyes closed. Do not stand up for a few minutes.

6. Do not worry about whether you are successful in achieving a deep level of relaxation. Maintain a passive attitude and permit relaxation to occur at its own pace. When distracting thoughts occur, try to ignore them by not dwelling upon them, and return to repeating one.

7. Practice once or twice daily, but ideally not within two hours after any meal, since digestive processes seem to interfere with elicitation of relaxation responses.

You may have noticed that this exercise is very much like meditation. In fact, meditation has provided the principles of the relaxation response. There is no need to spend several hundred dollars to learn to meditate. You now know all the steps.

GUIDED IMAGERY

A third relaxation technique is called "guided imagery." This is like a guided daydream where you transport yourself to another time and place. It is as though you were taking a mental stroll. The two guided imagery scripts presented here can be used in several different ways, depending on what works best for you. Consider each of the following techniques:

1. Read a script over several times to familiarize yourself with it. Then sit or lay in a quiet place and try to reconstruct the scene in your mind. Each script should take ten to fifteen minutes to complete.

2. Have a family member or friend slowly read you the script. Every place there are dots, ". . . ," there should be a five- to ten-second pause.

3. Make a tape of the script and play it to yourself.

Guided Imagery 1

Before imagining or listening to this scene, close your eyes and take three deep breaths . . . breathe slowly, and easily, in through your nose, out through your mouth . . .

Now picture a happy pleasant time in your life . . . a time when you had little or no problems with your arthritis . . .

Fill in the details of that time. . . . Look at your surroundings — indoors? outdoors . . . who was there? . . . what were you doing? . . . listen to the noises . . . even those in the background . . . are there any pleasant smells? . . . feel the temperature . . . now just enjoy your surroundings . . . you are happy . . . your body feels good . . . enjoy your surroundings . . . fix this feeling in your mind . . . you can return any time you wish by just picturing this happy time . . .

When you are ready, take three deep breaths . . . with each breath say the word "relax" and imagine the word written in the warm sand and open your eyes — remain quiet for a few moments before slowly returning to your activities.

Guided Imagery 2

Close your eyes and take three deep breaths . . . breathe slowly, and easily, in through your nose and out through your mouth . . .

Imagine yourself on a country road . . . the sun is warm on your back, the birds are singing . . . as you progress down the road, you come to a wooden gate . . . open it and enter . . . you are surrounded by an overgrown garden, roses climbing over a fallen tree, green grass, shade trees . . . smell the roses . . . listen to the birds . . . you walk down a cool damp path . . . the dense trees almost blot out the sun . . . feel the cool damp air . . . notice the moss . . . listen to a brook . . . now in the distance you hear a waterfall . . . soon the path breaks into a sunlit clearing, to the right is the cascade of water, there is a rainbow in the mist . . , you feel good enjoying the warmth and solitude of this peaceful place . . . it is now time to return, back down the path, one last smell of roses and out the wooden gate . . .

This secret garden is awaiting your return whenever you wish.

Now, take three deep breaths . . . with each breath say the word "relax" and imagine the word *relax* written in warm sand and open your eyes whenever you wish.

Remain quiet for a few moments before slowly returning to your activities.

VIVID IMAGERY

This is a little like guided imagery but can be used for longer periods and also while you are engaged in other activities.

One way to use imagery is to recall pleasant scenes from your past. For example, try to remember every detail of a special holiday or party that made you happy. Who was there? What happened? What did you talk about? Of course, you can do the same sort of thing with a vacation. Another way to use imagery is to fill in the details of a pleasant fantasy. How would you spend a million dollars? What would be your ideal romantic encounter? What would your ideal home or garden be like?

Sometimes warm imagery can be especially helpful, such as thinking of yourself on a warm beach or visiting a tropical island.

Another form of vivid imagery is to think of symbols that represent painful parts of your body. For example, a painful joint might be red or might have a tight band around it or even a lion biting it.

Now try to change the image. Make the red fade until there is no color left or imagine the band stretching and stretching until it falls off. Change the lion into a purring kitten.

A final way to use vivid imagery is to help with goal setting. After you set your weekly goal, take a few minutes to imagine yourself taking a walk, doing your exercises, or just taking your medications. Studies have shown that these few minutes of imagery will help you accomplish your goal. Many people become very skilled at vivid imagery. They find that as they change their pain images, the pain decreases.

BREATHING EXERCISES

These are really a special form of relaxation. You should concentrate on your breathing, taking a long slow breath through your nose, holding it for a few seconds, and breathing out through your mouth. As you do this say "relax" to yourself. You can try to focus the breath either at the back of your chest or, if you wish, on your painful joint. The most important thing is to concentrate on your breathing and keep it slow and easy. To check this, you might place a lit candle in front of you. When blowing out a breath, you should make the candle flicker but not go out.

One problem with breathing exercises is that sometimes people hyperventilate. That is, they have a hard time catching their breath. Hyperventilation is scary but not dangerous. Strangely enough, it is caused by having too much oxygen and not enough carbon dioxide. An easy way to restore the balance is to breathe into a closed paper bag for a *short* time.

Better yet, don't hyperventilate. By keeping your breathing slow and easy, you can completely avoid this problem.

DISSOCIATION

This technique involves mentally separating yourself from the painful part of your body. It is especially effective when pain is so severe that it is impossible to distract yourself.

To use dissociation, picture that the painful part of your body is separate from the rest of your body. Imagine that this body part is completely insensitive and therefore does not feel any pain. For example, tell yourself that your joint does not belong to you; it is completely separate from you. You cannot feel anything that happens to it. Whatever happens to your joint does not affect you at all. You can even imagine that you have floated away from your body and are looking at it from across the room.

PRAYER

Over the years, we have had many people tell us that prayer has been very helpful in managing their pain. In many ways, prayer is similar to some relaxation techniques, and in other ways, it may be a dissociation technique. However, one does not need to have a scientific rationale for everything. As the oldest of all pain-management techniques, prayer is very important for many successful arthritis pain managers.

DISTRACTION

Because our minds have trouble focusing on more than one thing at a time, you can lessen pain by focusing on something else. This technique can be especially helpful if you are going to do some activity you know to be painful, such as climbing stairs or opening a jar. Following are some suggestions for practicing distraction, also called "attention refocusing."

1. While climbing stairs, plan exactly what you will be doing when you get to the top. Be as detailed as possible. Or you might name a different bird or flower for each step. You can even try to visualize a bird or flower for every letter of the alphabet.

2. During any painful activity, try to think of a person's name, a bird, a food, or whatever, for every letter of the alphabet. If you get stuck on one letter, go on to the next. (This is also a good exercise if you have problems sleeping.)

3. While sweeping, vacuuming, or mopping, imagine that the floor is a map of the United States. Try to name all the states and their capitals going from east to west or north to south. You can also do this with the map of Europe, or if you are really good in geography, Africa. If geography is not your strong suit, think of your favorite store and where each of the departments is located.

4. When getting up from a chair or out of a car, imagine that you are in a spaceship where you are almost weightless, floating effortlessly upward. Or, you can try counting backward from 1,000 by threes, each time getting as far as you can until you have stood up. Try to break your old record.

5. While opening a jar, try to think of as many uses as you can for the jar. Or, try to remember the words of a song and imagine the story taking place inside the jar. Of course, you can add a million variations now that you have the refocusing idea.

So far we have discussed short-term refocusing strategies. However, this same technique works for long-term projects as well. Find an activity that really interests you and you will find yourself distracted from your pain. This activity can be almost anything, from cooking or stamp collecting to watching a movie or doing volunteer work. One of the marks of a successful arthritis manager is that he or she has a variety of interests and always seems to be doing something.

RELABELING

This technique is almost the opposite of distraction, or attention refocusing. Rather than thinking of something else, you think about your pain. However, you do more than you think. You try to analyze the pain. Is it sharp, dull, hot, cold? Exactly what are the sensations that you are feeling? Now, concentrate on your pulse or muscle tension in or around your joint, but don't think of "pain." Think of the various sensations. These sensations may increase, decrease, or level off. Just go along with them. See if you can begin to think of the sensations as mere dullness, as if the joint had become completely numb.

SELF-TALK — "I KNOW I CAN"

Most of us remember the story of the little train going up the hill saying "I think I can, I think I can." This is an excellent example of self-talk. Tell yourself that you *can* do things. Try to get rid of negative and "can't" thoughts.

Sometimes a little song or rhyme will help. A woman in one of our classes with very painful knees says to herself, "Right foot up, left foot down, now I'm moving closer to town." Of course when her shopping is done, she says "Left foot up, right foot down, now I'm moving toward home." These phrases are repeated until she gets where she is going.

Just remember the little engine that could, and say "I know I can, I know I can. . . ."

HYPNOSIS

Many of the techniques discussed in this chapter are similar to those used in self-hypnosis. However, hypnosis, other than self-hypnosis, is not generally recommended for people with arthritis, because like certain narcotics, it can mask pain and cause you to inadvertently damage your joints.

SKIN STIMULATION

Sometimes pain can be decreased by stimulating the skin over the painful area. This stimulation can be done with heat, such as a hotpad or a warm bath or shower (directed at the sore area). Some people prefer cold for soothing pain. A bag of frozen peas or corn makes an inexpensive, reusable ice pack. Whether using heat or cold, do it for fifteen to twenty minutes.

Another way to stimulate the skin is by using a counterirritant such as any of the mentholated creams, which give a cooling effect.

Finally, many people find that massage or rubbing the painful area can be very helpful. Massage is actually one of the oldest forms of pain management for arthritis. Hippocrates (c.460–380 B.C.) said that "physicians must be experienced in many things, but assuredly also in rubbing that can bind a joint that is loose and loosen a joint that is too hard." Self-massage is a simple procedure that can be performed with little practice or preparation. It stimulates the skin, underlying tissues, and muscles by means of applied pressure and stretching.

Massage is not appropriate on a "hot joint," an infected joint, or one that is suffering from phlebitis, thrombophlebitis, or skin eruptions. Following are some basic massage techniques to practice. A little experience will help you decide which works best for you.

After any kind of self-massage, allow yourself a minute to relax and let the tension subside. Breathe deeply.

Stroking

Fit your hand to the contour of the muscle you want to massage and move it over the skin. By slightly cupping the hand, the palm and fingers will glide firmly over the muscle. A slow rhythmic movement repeated over the tense or sore area works best. Experiment with different pressures.

Kneading

If you have ever reached up and squeezed your tense neck or shoulder muscles, you were kneading. As if you were kneading dough, grasp the muscle between the palm and fingers or between the thumb and fingers, then slightly lift and squeeze it. Don't pinch the skin, but work more deeply into the muscle itself. A slow, rhythmic squeeze and release works best. Don't knead one spot for more than fifteen or twenty seconds.

Deep Circular Movement or Friction

To create friction that penetrates into the muscle, make small circular movements with the tips of the fingers, the thumb, or the heel or the hand, depending on how large an area you want to massage. Keeping the fingers, thumb, or palm in one place, begin lightly making small circles and slowly increase the pressure. Don't overdo it. After ten seconds or so, move to another spot and repeat.

A WORD OF CAUTION

The pain management techniques taught in this chapter, along with such other techniques as hypnosis, self-hypnosis, biofeedback, and acupressure, are not "scientifically proven" treatments for arthritis, and we make no special claims for them. Many people in our classes report substantial benefits from these practices, however, and we feel that they have merit if used as an adjunct to and not a substitute for a basic, sound program that is medically directed.

Unfortunately, various pain-management techniques are sold in expensive packages as cure-alls for almost everything. Such expensive courses and treatments are *not* necessary. If you want to further explore these techniques, check the following points to avoid unnecessary expense and disappointment.

1. Is the course or treatment offered by a reputable institution?

2. Is the cost reasonable (five to ten dollars for each hour of small group instruction is about average)?

3. Are claims or promises made for a cure? If so, look elsewhere.

9

Outsmarting Arthritis

Pain, fatigue, and stiffness are affects of arthritis that can limit you in a variety of ways. They may prevent you from completing a specific task, hinder the progress of your daily activities, or even leave you feeling completely overwhelmed. From simple physical tasks such as unlocking doors, opening jars, or getting on buses to social activities, arthritis can interfere with your life. For example, you may find yourself avoiding new places because you do not know if there will be an accessible bathroom and fear of fatigue may prevent you from entertaining. As you will discover in this book, exercise, pain-management techniques, and medications can help to alleviate the symptoms of arthritis. In this chapter, you will find a problem-solving approach to overcoming obstacles that you may encounter in your everyday life, including strategies for using your joints appropriately and labor-saving ideas and products that can make your daily activities easier and more pleasant. But before discussing strategies for outsmarting arthritis, it might help to define pain, fatigue, and stiffness.

1. **Pain.**   For the person with arthritis, pain can occur for different reasons. These include active inflammation of a joint, exercising muscles that are not frequently used, or overstressing joints. Performing a stressful activity for long periods of time will increase the likelihood of pain. For example, writing a letter for five minutes may cause stress in the fingers but no pain. Continuing to write for an hour might cause pain that lasts for two or three days. Too much body weight increases the load on joints, as does carrying heavy objects or performing activities that require you to work against gravity, such as climbing stairs, getting up from a chair, and carrying heavy grocery bags.

It is important to respect pain. Pain is the best indication of excess joint stress and serves as a warning sign for you to modify your activities.

2. **Fatigue.**   Fatigue is a common human experience. It occurs when certain basic needs are not met. For example, not getting proper food, enough sleep, or enough exercise. It can result from inflamed joints or even from depression.

Too much activity will also cause fatigue. What is too much? For some people, running five miles a day is not enough to tire them out, but for others, doing three loads of laundry, standing on the bus during rush hour, or climbing a full flight of stairs may cause fatigue. It's important to know your limits and work within them. In this way, they will gradually increase. Knowing limits is crucial for someone with arthritis. For example, you must be particularly careful not to overdo it when you're beginning to feel good again after an episode of pain. This can cause fatigue or more pain. If you feel fatigued often, consider your diet (see Chapter 13), your sleeping habits (see Chapter 11), and make sure that you are getting enough, but not too much, exercise (see Chapter 7).

3. **Stiffness.**   Stiffness is the inability to move your joints and muscles easily. Arthritis contributes to stiffness. Arthritis-induced stiffness can be aggravated by maintaining one position for too long while writing, reading, chopping food, or participating in other repetitive activities. Sitting in a movie theater, traveling long distances in a car or plane, and sleeping will also make your body feel stiff.

Other factors contributing to stiffness are pain and the lack of strengthening exercise. When you experience pain, the natural reaction is to try to eliminate it. Protecting a joint by keeping it bent may offer temporary relief, but in the long run, it will cause more stiffness, and

possible contractures, or permanent limitation of joint motion, resulting in the inability to fully bend or straighten a joint.

Pain, fatigue and stiffness may occur separately or in combination. A
good arthritis self-manager will be able to keep them all in check. However, left untreated, they can result in a cycle in which pain, fatigue,
and stiffness lead to an unwillingness to move, increased stiffness, and
shortening of muscles and joint tissues, resulting in more pain and limited movement. Don't contribute to your pain, fatigue, and stiffness by
ignoring them. Also take care not to overprotect joints, because this too
can lead to increased problems.

STEPS TO DISABILITY

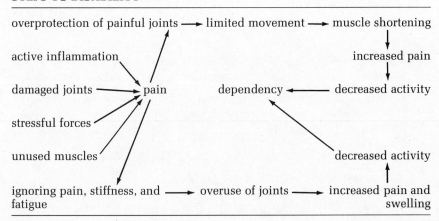

Now that you know about pain, fatigue, and stiffness, the next step
is to identify how they factor into your daily activities.

PROBLEM-SOLVING METHOD

Many of the problems caused by arthritis can be solved with the eight-
step plan: *identify, pinpoint, list, select, assess, substitute, utilize resources, and accept.*

1. **Identify the source of difficulty.** This is the most important step and
   probably the most difficult. This step needs to be broken down to
   help you zero in on the true source of the problem.

- *Identify specific activities that cause you pain, stiffness, or fatigue.*

  If you are having trouble identifying activities that cause problems, review the past 24 hours, using the following method:

- List your activities.

- Check off activities that have caused pain in the past.

- Circle new activities.

- Look at the checked and circled activities. Repeat those so you can see if you reproduce the symptoms. (Do not overdo the repetition.)

  Ask yourself if this is more or less activity than you usually do in a day.

- Did your activities keep your joints in one position for long periods?

- If none of the above help you identify the problem, ask yourself: "Are my joints red, hot, and swollen? Could my arthritis be in an active state? Are my basic needs being met? Am I under extra stress/tension?"

2. **Now, pinpoint the source of the problem.**

- What part of the activity caused pain or stiffness?

- When did fatigue begin?

- Consider stress, speed at which you worked, and duration of the task.

  Pinpoint an activity that you would like to do but feel you cannot. Why can't you do the activity? Is it due to decreased motion, pain, fatigue, stiffness, or weakness? Is your participation being limited by a fear of how others will perceive you?

3. **List** ideas that might solve your problem. If you are short of ideas, ask family or friends for suggestions.

4. **Select** an idea that you think will work, and try it out.

5. **Assess** the results. Did you feel that the problem was completely solved or was it a partial solution? If you still have problems, try the next step.

6. **Substitute** another idea from your list if the first one did not work. Continue to substitute until you exhaust all your ideas.

7. **Utilize resources.** If you exhaust your own ideas without solving the problem, use the following resources: health professionals, books, and the Arthritis Foundation.

8. **Accept** that the problem may not be solved at this time. Your present investigation may help you solve the problem or modify the activity in the future.

The following section will discuss techniques that will broaden your list of ideas, and provide you with greater ability to select likely solutions. They may also play a role in preventing future problems by showing you how to get the task done with the least amount of effort. At the end of the chapter, you will find examples of common problems and their solutions using the method described above.

BODY MECHANICS

The principle of body mechanics is to use your muscles and joints efficiently in order to reduce stress, pain, and fatigue. Proper attention to these principles can solve many potential problems.

> # 1. Distribute the load over stronger joint(s) and/or larger surface area

PURPOSE

- To reduce joint stress and prevent joint pain by spreading the weight of objects you are carrying, pushing, or pulling.

- To eliminate tight grasping and pinching since they may stress your knuckles or cause hand stiffness. If you notice deformities developing in your hand(s), ask your doctor about consultation with an occupational therapist. A management program can be developed to meet your specific needs.

EXAMPLES

- Instead of using your fingers, use the palms of your hand, your forearms, or your elbows; instead of your arms, use your whole body; instead of your back, use your legs.

Wrong

Right

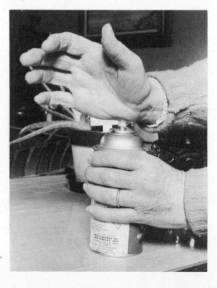

When using spray cans or bottles, push down with the palm of the hand instead of the thumb tip.

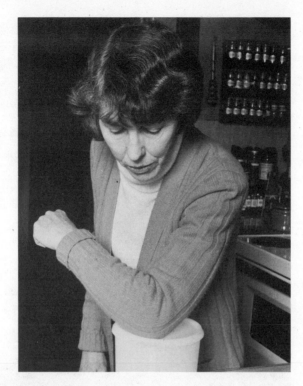

Close plastic containers with your elbow.

Wring out wet washcloths or laundry by wrapping the item over the faucet and squeezing excess water out between the palms of your hands. An alternative is to wrap the item in a thick towel and let the towel soak up the excess moisture.

Spare your hands from difficult-to-open refrigerator doors or cupboards by placing a strap on the handle. To open, simply place your forearm through the strap and pull.

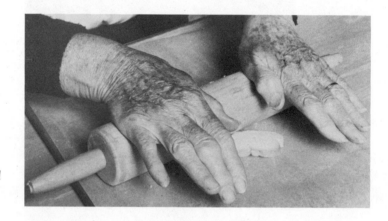

Instead of holding onto the handles of a rolling pin, place hands flat on top and roll beneath your hands.

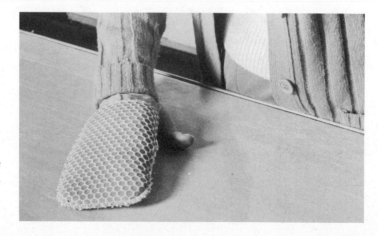

To wash dishes, there is a scrubber that fits over your hand available in supermarkets or hardware stores. Since you don't need to grasp it, you can keep your fingers in a straightened position.

Use a sponge instead of a dishrag to mop up tables and counters. The water can be squeezed out of the sponge more easily by putting it in the sink and pressing down with your flattened hand.

Wrong

Right

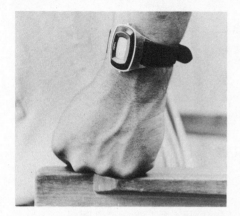

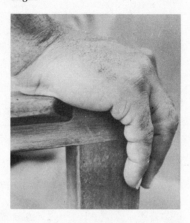

When pushing up from a chair, keep your hands facing palm down.

Use your hip to close kitchen or dresser drawers.

Use both arms to take down or hang clothes in the closet.

Instead of placing your fingers through the handle, encircle a coffee cup with both hands. Mugs are especially good for this.

Carry your plate back to the kitchen by "scooping" it up with the palms of both hands.

2. Use body leverage

PURPOSE

Holding objects close to your body will reduce the load, which will in turn reduce fatigue and joint stress. Objects feel heavier if held farther away from your body, and lighter when held closer.

EXAMPLES

Carrying a briefcase, use a shoulder strap — avoid using the handles. Carry a purse on your forearm or use a shoulder bag to avoid clutching in your hand.

Right

Holding a brown paper grocery bag close to body with both arms

Wrong

Holding a plastic grocery bag with hand down at the side of body

3. Avoid maintaining the same joint position for prolonged periods

PURPOSE

- To reduce joint stiffness
- To prevent joint contractures

EXAMPLES

Hips and Knees

Alternate between sitting and standing positions. Although the sitting position is generally recommended to reduce stress on the lower joints and prevent fatigue, it is important to get up and stretch frequently.

A book holder or pillows on your lap will serve as a means to support a book and will free your hands.

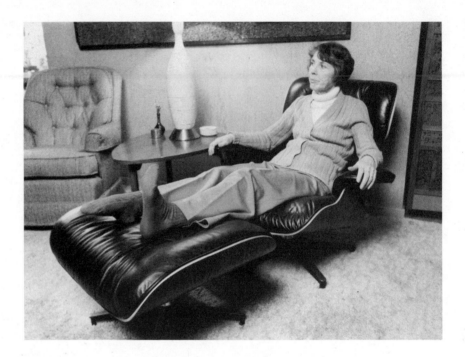

Knees

When sitting, change the position of your legs so that your knees are often stretched out, feet supported by a footstool.

Ankles

Bend and point your toes while watching television or talking with a friend. You don't have to wait for a specific exercise time to do your range-of-motion exercises.

Hands

Avoid sustained grasps on objects. For example, instead of writing with a pen, use a typewriter or a word processor.

---

4. Reduce excess body weight

PURPOSE

- To reduce stress on joints and fatigue see Chapter 13.

5. Use good posture

PURPOSE

Proper body alignment in standing, sitting, lifting, and when changing positions uses your muscles and joints more efficiently.

EXAMPLES

Pelvic Tilt

This exercise, which is a key component of posture, was described in Chapter 7 (exercise 28). The degree that the pelvis is tilted in relation to the spine helps determine how straight the spine is aligned. The better the alignment, the less strain on both muscles and joints.

 To feel this position, please refer to exercise 28 on page 63. While doing these exercises, focus your awareness on the trunk and hips and try to maintain this position, the pelvic tilt, later during the day.

 To practice a pelvic tilt while standing, pretend you have a long tail. Bring the tail between your legs and hold it at belt level. Now pull straight up. Feel your pelvis tilt.

Standing

When standing for prolonged periods of time is necessary, alternate your position between the examples that follow.

Sitting

Position your body as follows:

- upper back straight

- knees slightly higher than hips

- forearms resting on work surface or arm rest

- shoulders relaxed not elevated

- lower back flattened with a pelvic tilt

- buttocks flat on seat

- feet flat on floor or some surface

At right: Stand with weight distributed equally between both feet. For a back problem, to assist with maintaining the pelvic tilt, avoid locking your knees. Don't do this if you also have a knee problem.

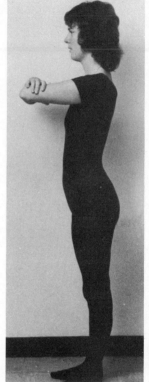 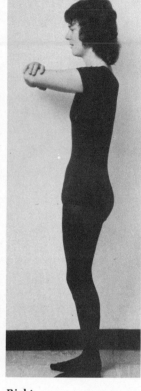

Wrong   **Right**

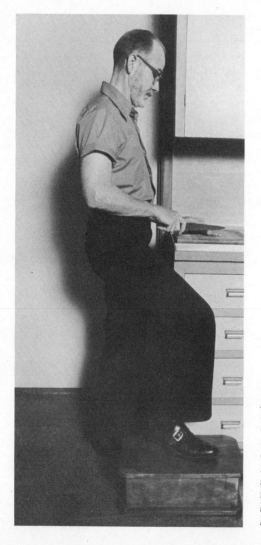

Place one foot on a footstool. This helps to maintain a pelvic tilt and thus alleviate low back strain. Wear flat or low-heeled shoes, not only for the greater stability and safety they afford, but also because they help to keep the pelvis tilted.

Select a chair that:

- has a firm seat

- has a fairly straight back

- is the right height for the work surface, in order to allow you to position your body as stated above

When working at your workbench or in the kitchen, a bar-height stool with footrest allows you to half-sit, half-stand. This helps to prevent fatigue, as well as to provide a suitable height for working on projects, washing dishes, or preparing meals.

When writing at a desk, do not lean forward, but sit tall and bend the neck only slightly.

Persons with neck problems may want to consider a drafting table with an adjustable slant.

Working at a computer terminal requires the terminal to be at a correct height and a chair with good back support. If a proper chair is not available, try a small pillow for the lower back.

Standing Up

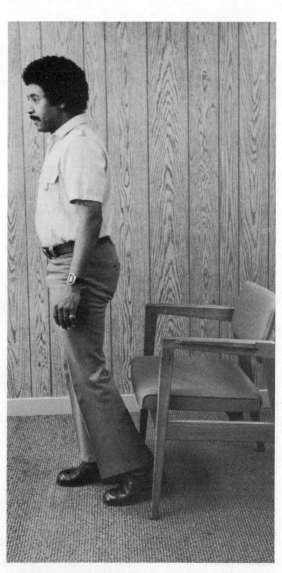

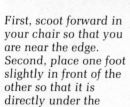

First, scoot forward in your chair so that you are near the edge. Second, place one foot slightly in front of the other so that it is directly under the

knee. The other foot is behind the knee. Then lean forward until your hips automatically start to come off the chair.

Chairs that are several inches higher than normal, either through the use of pillows or chair leg extenders, make it easier to stand up.

Lifting

Wrong

To lift objects from the ground or low shelves, bend your legs instead of your back; pick up the object, holding it as close to your body as possible, and rise, letting your leg muscles do the work.

Right

Persons with knee involvement may want to let someone else lift heavy objects, since the knees will be strained from the weight of the object as well as from their own body weight.

Getting Up from the Floor

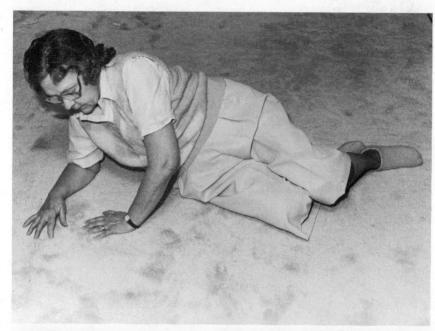

1. Roll onto one side.

2. With the upper hand, push yourself up enough to get your lower elbow under you.

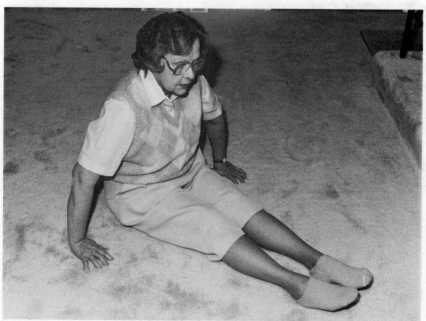

3. Gradually rise until you are sitting up.

4. Reach across your body until both hands are on the floor at one side.

5. Shift your weight sideways; tuck your knees under and get up onto all fours.

6. Crawl to the nearest steady chair and place your hands on the seat for support.

7. Putting weight onto your hands, bring one knee up and put that foot flat. (If you have one leg stronger than the other, the strong leg should be in the position of "foot flat" — ready to push up.)

8. Push up with that leg, bearing much of your weight on your hands as they rest on the chair.

9. *When you have straightened your legs, stop, keep your head down and let your circulation catch up with the change of positions.*

10. *Now, stand up fully straight. But again, stop a moment before you start to walk to let your circulation adjust; many people become dizzy if they get up too fast.*

EFFICIENCY PRINCIPLES

When you plan and organize your tasks and workspaces, you often reduce unnecessary steps and save time and energy. This helps reduce fatigue. Hasty movements are no more quickly accomplished than organized movements, and they often end in extra work. As the adage says, "Haste makes waste." Both tension and fatigue are increased when we feel rushed.

1. Plan

DETERMINE THE FOLLOWING

- Is the task necessary?
- Can the task be simplified?
- Who should perform the task?
- What steps are involved in completing the task?

- In what order will these steps be most efficient?

- What is the best time of day or week to perform the task?

- Do you need rest periods to complete the task?

- What is the best body position to use to complete the task?

EXAMPLES

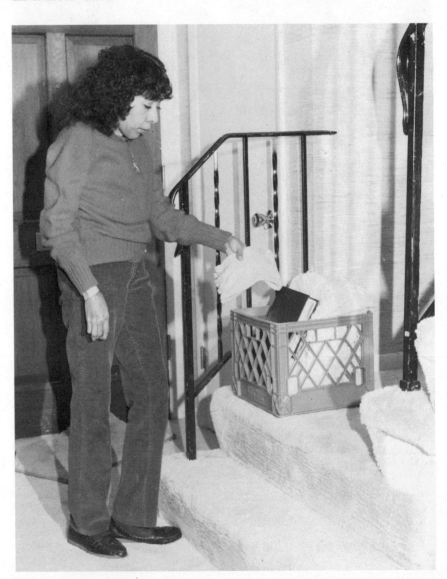

Combine several errands in one trip whenever possible. If you have to go downstairs or to another part of the house or place of work, try to accomplish several things at a time.

Work in an assembly-line basis. First gather all items you need to complete the task and place them at your workspace. Choose a comfortable position to work, then work in the order most efficient.

2. Organize

ORGANIZE IN THE FOLLOWING WAY

- Store equipment and supplies that are regularly used between eye and hip level to minimize bending, stooping, and needless searching. Store the heavier items in easy reach, such as on countertops.

- Eliminate clutter. Remove unnecessary or infrequently used items from shelves.

- Duplicate inexpensive items in places where most frequently used.

EXAMPLES

A hint to remove clutter: Put items you do not use in a bin. If you do not look for these in a month, get rid of them.

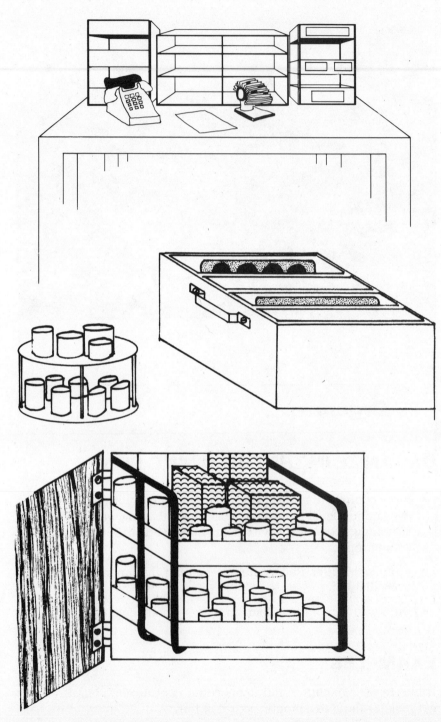

Organize storage areas with dividers, special racks, turntables, and pull-out shelves. Many of these items are available in local stores or can be easily made by a carpenter.

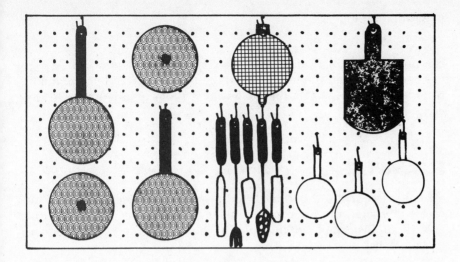

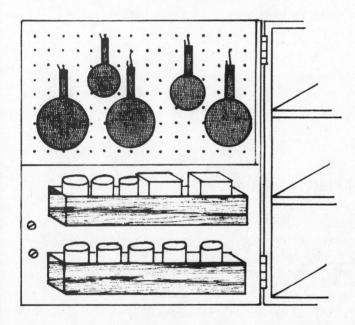

Use pegboards and hooks to hang objects.

3. Balance work with rest

PURPOSE

One of the most effective means of avoiding fatigue is to schedule short but frequent rest periods throughout the day. Resting before you get tired is often difficult because we all want to get our work done. If we can prevent fatigue, even if it means stopping in the middle of a job, our endurance over the long run will be increased. While stopping to rest is difficult, remember that long work periods require longer recovery periods.

EXAMPLES

Schedule frequent rest periods throughout the day. These will vary for each individual, but an example might be to rest ten minutes out of every hour, instead of working for three hours straight. Even a momentary break is better than nothing.

Alternate heavy and light work tasks during each day. In addition, plan the more difficult or lengthy tasks when you know you have the endurance to do them.

Sitting to work is a form of rest since it uses less energy than standing. However, if you spend your workday behind a desk, you will find that moving around at regular intervals will help to keep you more alert and energetic.

PRODUCT SELECTION PRINCIPLES

Using products with the features described in this section will help reduce joint stress, pain, and fatigue by allowing you to complete a task with the least amount of effort. These principles will help you choose new products and evaluate those you already own.

1. Use wheels

PURPOSE

- To reduce friction, lessening the resistance between surfaces
- To avoid lifting and carrying

EXAMPLES

At left: Use a luggage carrier or suitcase on wheels when traveling. This allows you to take most of the strain off your arms as you push or pull the suitcase.

At right: "Deluxe" trash cans are now available that come equipped with wheels and a push handle. In addition, trash toters also have wheels in front and generally hold two regular-size trash cans.

Use wheels to transport. Utility carts, tea tables, and shopping carts are just a few examples of readily available items on wheels.

2. Use levers

PURPOSE

Products with long handles or long attachments will enable you to manipulate objects using less force. These products will help to conserve your strength.

EXAMPLES

A piece of wood, metal, or firm plastic can be attached to many types of objects to increase the area for gripping.

A doorknob extender allows you to open the door with the palm of the hand instead of with the fingers.

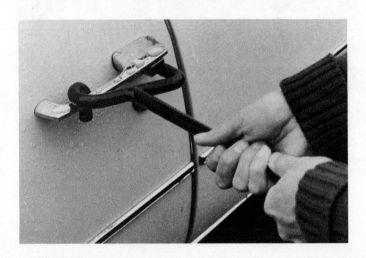

Open a car door with an aid in the palm of your hand.

Special key holder devices allow you to turn a key by holding the handle in the palm of your hand. These are available through special-equipment firms or can be made by riveting a piece of wood or metal to the key.

Attach a dowel or a piece of wood to a can opener and hold onto this lengthened handle when opening cans. Never use a butterfly can opener, because the pressure required to operate them is extreme; use an electric or wall-mounted type.

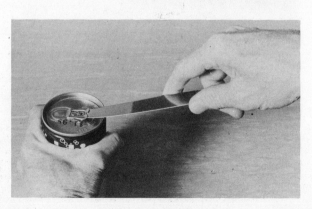

Open ring or flip-top cans with a knife.

---

3. Use lightweight objects

PURPOSE

- To reduce joint stress and pain and fatigue

EXAMPLES

Items	Lightweight brands	What to avoid
dishes	plastic Corelle Heller	stoneware
pots/pans	Metrolight Prochief Frazier	iron skillet
bowls	plastic aluminum	Pyrex stoneware
baking dishes casseroles	foil pans aluminum microwave cookware Farberware T-fal	Corningware
luggage/briefcases	nylon canvas	leather hardback
fans	plastic	metal
winter coats	fiberfill goose down	leather wool

---

4. Use enlarged handles

PURPOSE

- To help maintain a secure hold when hands are weak
- To help hold an object if fingers do not fully close
- To lessen tension required to maintain your hold on objects

EXAMPLES

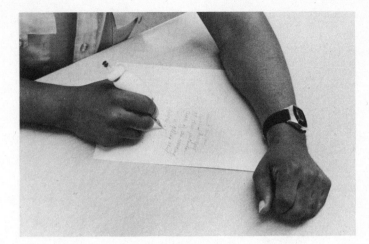

Foam padding added to such articles as a toothbrush, pen, razor, fork, and comb will increase the size of the handle.

---

5. Use convenience items

PURPOSE

- To decrease the length of time and number of steps needed to complete task
- To reduce joint stress and pain and fatigue

EXAMPLES

Use labor-saving devices, such as food processor, blender, microwave, electric toothbrush, prepared foods, electric hedger, and permanent press clothing.

PUTTING IT ALL TOGETHER

Now you have all the information you need to apply the problem-solving method to some of the problems interfering with your daily routine. Here are some examples of how the problem-solving method is used. It is important to note that the solution to each problem varies from case to case, depending on the situations surrounding the problem.

Example 1

IDENTIFY:	I can't open jars.
PINPOINT:	It sometimes causes pain; I'm too weak.
LIST:	Ask husband or neighbor. Use cans and open with electric can opener. Buy commercial jar opener. Use sheet of rubber to reduce friction by placing over lid. Release suction with a knife. Tap jar upside down.
SELECT:	Tried to release suction.
ASSESS:	Worked on some jars but not others.
SUBSTITUTE:	Buy commercial jar opener.
ASSESS:	It's wonderful!

Example 2

IDENTIFY:	My joints are red, hot, and swollen. Activities seem to make them worse. My doctor says rest and do what I can.
LIST:	Stay in bed. Keep up my regular routine. Meet basic needs by getting sufficient sleep, eat well, reduce tension as possible, and exercise appropriately. Decrease activities that can wait. Delegate tasks, modify tasks.
SELECT:	Stay in bed.
ASSESS:	Stayed in bed and did not move for two days. I feel less fatigue, but my joints are stiff. I think I lost strength.
SUBSTITUTE:	Try three ideas at once: meet basic needs, decrease activities that can wait, and delegate tasks or modify tasks.
ASSESS:	I feel better. In order to reduce tension, I stopped all activities that can wait, and delegated tasks to family and friends. I move my joints twice a day and feel less stiff. I still shower and dress daily. *Note:* This period of active arthritis seemed milder than usual.

Example 3

IDENTIFY:	I can't go on vacation.
PINPOINT:	I can't walk long distances in airport. How will I find accessible bathrooms?

LIST:	Bring raised toilet seat.
	Call hotel in advance regarding bathrooms.
	Call travel agent.
	Contact airlines regarding wheelchair.
SELECT:	Call travel agent.
ASSESS:	Travel agent booked me on an airline with wheelchair service from cab to plane. She contacted the hotel and investigated bathroom status. I still need to bring my raised toilet seat.

Example 4

IDENTIFY:	My body aches after working at my desk for an hour.
PINPOINT:	Suspect desk is too high.
LIST:	Elevate chair by adding cushion.
	Work at different location with a lower table.
	Purchase new chair.
SELECT:	Add cushion.
ASSESS:	The cushion improved the work height but now my feet are off the floor. I added a small block under my feet which helped tremendously.

Example 5

IDENTIFY:	I have joint pain during intercourse.
LIST:	Grin and bear it.
	Make up excuses to avoid.
	Find resources to learn new positions, i.e., call Arthritis Foundation.
	Discuss with mate.
SELECT:	Grin and bear it.
ASSESS:	Pain increased and now I am making excuses. My husband seems frustrated.
SUBSTITUTE:	Call Arthritis Foundation, ask for name of resources.
ASSESS:	Received a copy of "Living and Loving." Tried suggestions in the book and my husband noticed the difference. I admitted my pain and we are reviewing other resources together.

Example 6

IDENTIFY:	I am afraid to visit friends for brunch. How will I use the toilet?

LIST:	Stay home.
	Bring raised toilet seat.
	Call friend and ask about her toilet accessibility.
	Use toilet before leaving, bring raised toilet seat but leave in car.
SELECT:	Call friend and ask about toilet height.
ASSESS:	Friend suggested I come early and bring toilet seat before other guests arrive to avoid embarrassment. She will store it in the bathroom closet.

Example 7

IDENTIFY:	My knees feel stiff and sore after sitting in a movie theater.
	Walk to lobby once an hour.
	Sit in aisle seat and stretch legs every fifteen minutes.
	Sit in last row and stand when I need to.
SELECT:	Walk to lobby once an hour.
ASSESS:	This wasn't often enough to decrease stiffness. I felt embarrassed to get up more than that.
SUBSTITUTE:	Sit in aisle seat and stretch legs every fifteen minutes.
ASSESS:	This helped, but I decided every ten minutes worked better for me.

Example 8

IDENTIFY:	I have trouble unlocking doors.
PINPOINT:	My fingers are too weak to turn keys. Repeated attempts hurt my fingers.
LIST:	Oil lock.
	Lengthen area to grasp — add lever.
	Ask in hardware store if larger keys are available.
SELECT:	Add lever.
ASSESS:	Attached key to piece of plastic with wire. I can open the door on the first or second attempt.

Example 9

IDENTIFY:	I'm exhausted when I carry groceries. Sometimes my back hurts.
LIST:	Carry smaller loads.
	Hold groceries closer to body.

	Seek assistance: ask family or friend, pay to have groceries delivered. Use pelvic tilt when carrying groceries. Use cart or wagon. Use backpack.
SELECT:	Seek assistance.
ASSESS:	Worked well first time, but my friend seemed to resent the third consecutive week and refused.
SUBSTITUTE:	Carry smaller loads and hold close to body.
ASSESS:	Able to manage one bag half-filled. Contacted friend and asked for help once a month. She said yes. Combining both ideas seems to work well.

10

Self-Helpers
100 Plus Hints and Aids

The preceding chapter on outsmarting arthritis provided you with basic principles and examples of how to protect your joints. Additional hints are provided in this chapter, not only on how to use your joints appropriately, but also on how to perform activities if your general mobility or finger coordination are impaired.

You may find that you already use many of the suggestions listed below. It is true that necessity is the mother of invention. If you combine your needs and your common sense, you will probably come up with another 100 hints. Use the suggestions here as a springboard for additional ideas to make your life easier and more comfortable. Then share them with friends and others who also could benefit from them.

DRESSING

If buttons are difficult to manipulate, sew Velcro on clothing, attach buttons permanently to the top side, and use the Velcro as a fastener. Velcro can be found in most sewing stores.

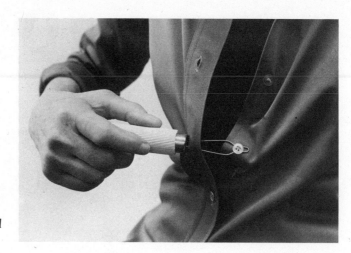

Buttonhooks work well to fasten buttons.

An alternative for buttons on sleeves is to sew elasticized thread on button cuffs. This often provides sufficient give for your hands to slide through.

In the future, buy clothes that are easy to put on and easy to care for. Tops should be large enough or designed so that sleeves are easy to slip into — you may want to avoid turtlenecks. Elastic waistbands around pants should be loose enough to slip easily over hips. Fastenings should be located in the front and be easy to manipulate.

If reaching the clothes in the closet is difficult, have someone lower the rod.

Special devices to assist with shoes include long-handled shoe horns, elastic shoelaces, and zipper laces.

A bent coat hanger, reacher, or dressing stick can assist with pulling pants up, straightening shirts, or retrieving clothes slightly out of reach.

Place large rings, thread, or leather loops on zipper tabs.

Fasten your bra in front of you. Turn bra around and pull it into place. Try front closure bras.

When putting on your girdle, first roll it down from the top to the bottom, then step in, pull it onto your hips, and unroll. Dusting your thighs with powder makes it easier for the girdle to be pulled into place. Try using this technique for pantyhose as well.

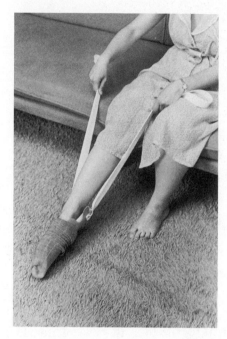

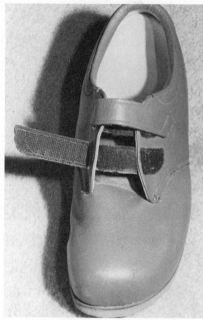

At far left: A stocking device will allow you to put socks on again if you can't reach your feet.

At left: Velcro can be useful for fastening shoes as well as other clothing.

SHOES

When buying shoes, look for the following characteristics:

1. low heel — no higher than 1 inch

2. toe area wide and deep enough to prevent rubbing or crunching of toes

3. cushion sole to pad the ball of your foot — avoid wood

4. laces or buckles to loosen or tighten when feet swell

5. soft upper material to give or be stretched to relieve pressure on specific areas.

Don't rule out gym shoes. Many of the running and aerobic shoes meet the above criteria. Some now have Velcro closures.

If your present shoes have the recommended characteristics but are still uncomfortable, consult your physician or podiatrist.

There are a variety of shoe adaptations available such as:

- soft cushion inserts
- custom-molded inserts
- pads for ball of foot
- external bar under shoe

Most of them take pressure off the ball of the foot. Consult your physician or podiatrist when choosing the proper adaptation for you. Foot problems are very individual.

BATHING AND HYGIENE

A long-handled sponge or brush can be used to soap yourself when bathing.

Tub and shower benches, or a webbed-plastic lawn chair, can allow you to sit while showering. This helps to prevent fatigue and provides a place to sit when getting down into the tub is difficult.

Safety considerations when bathing include the use of nonskid safety strips or a rubber bathmat on the floor. In addition, grab bars can be permanently installed on the wall or attached to the edge of the bathtub. Grab bars assist with safety when climbing in and out of the tub or shower and also provide a place to pull or push up from when in the tub.

A long shower spray hose makes rinsing easier.

After bathing, put on a terry robe and let it soak up the water as you pat yourself dry.

Use a shower caddy to keep soap and shampoo within easy reach.

In addition, a toilet safety frame or a grab bar installed in the wall next to the toilet will allow you to assist with your arms when sitting and standing.

Electric toothbrushes and Water-Piks make oral hygiene easier. In addition, there is a device that holds dental floss, allowing you to floss your teeth with one hand holding onto the handle — ask your dentist about these or check your local drugstore.

Special long-handled combs and brushes are useful when shoulder and elbow limitations prevent reaching your head.

Put foam curlers onto eyeliner and mascara handles for better grip.

Use the heel of your hand to squeeze the toothpaste tube or press down on a toothpaste pump.

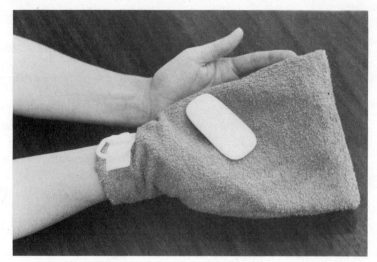

A bath mitt can be bought or easily made by sewing two facecloths together. Lather it up and soap yourself the easy way.

A raised toilet seat or commode over the toilet provides greater height and thus makes standing up easier.

COOKING

Microwave ovens save time and energy. They are easy to operate, easy to clean, and easy to reach since they are usually placed on counter-tops. In addition, you do not need to worry about burning yourself since only the food heats up.

To avoid lifting pots heavy with food and the water it was boiled in, there are several alternatives. One is to place a frying basket inside a pot so that you may lift the food out with the basket and drain the water later. Spaghetti cookers come with a perforated insert and can serve in the same manner. Or you may want to ladle the contents out.

To open jars, install a jar opener that will grip the lid as you use both hands to turn the jar itself. Also, ask other members of the family not to close lids too tightly.

Use lightweight cooking utensils, bowls, and dishes. Avoid cast-iron skillets and heavy ceramic bowls.

Use efficient storage arrangements.

Select appliances with levers or push buttons that are easy to operate.

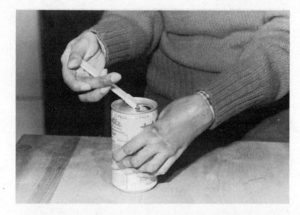

Opener for soda and beer cans

Jar opener

Store canned goods so that the same items are lined up behind one another. This way you can tell from the front label what is in the back of the shelf.

Plan and prepare meals ahead of time to avoid last-minute preparations. Cook some meals the day before, let the flavors enhance, and then heat them up again the next day. Also, try preparing double or triple portions and freeze the extra.

Use menus that require short preparation and little effort, e.g., frozen foods, convenience foods, and ready mixes.

One-pot meals require less cleanup.

Serve foods in the same containers in which they were cooked. Use casseroles, Farberware, and other lightweight, attractive cooking vessels.

Use pie tins and other throw-away utensils. This cuts down on dishwashing.

Line pans with aluminum foil to make cleanup easier.

Use cookie tins and pans with special surfaces that prevent sticking and messy cleanup, or spray them with a nonstick product.

Mixing bowls can be stabilized by placing on a wet washcloth or on little octopus suction cups. You can also place the bowl in a drawer at work height.

Place flour and sugar in containers so you can scoop out the amount needed and avoid lifting heavy bags each time.

Mitt pot holders allow you to lift hot pans with the palms of both hands.

Use a bent coat hanger or dowel with a hook to pull oven shelves out when checking on the meal.

Use a pot with a wet cloth draped over it as a support for a bowl when pouring batter into a baking pan.

When peeling vegetables, try the kind of peeler with a handle you can slip your fingers through or build up the handle of a standard peeler.

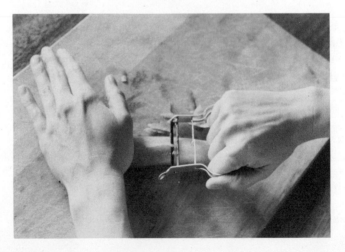

Attach a spray hose at the kitchen sink so that you can fill pots with water on the countertop; slide pots to the stove to avoid lifting.

Try using a pizza wheel to cut various foods.

Food processors make food preparation a snap, especially when large quantities of food must be chopped, sliced, or grated.

 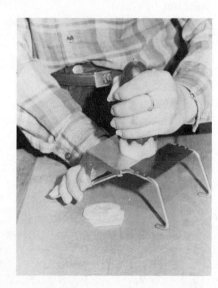

If you can't afford the electric food processors, use an onion chopper, or a Femster.

ENTERTAINING

Arrange a buffet meal. Let your guests select their own silver, plates, napkins, etc., and serve themselves from large dishes of food.

Use nice paper plates and plastic utensils to eliminate dish-washing.

Have a potluck meal, asking each guest to bring a dish of food or some paper goods.

HOUSEKEEPING

Keep a set of cleaning supplies in each area where they are used to eliminate needless walking.

To clean the bathtub, sit on a low stool next to the tub and use a long-handled sponge.

Long-handled sponges can also be used to clean around door sills and other hard-to-reach places.

Use a long-handled dustpan and small broom to clean up dry spills from floors.

Use an adjustable-height ironing board so that you can sit to iron. Attach a cord-minder to keep the cord out of your way.

Carpeting or foam-backed rugs help to ease ankle and foot pain when prolonged standing and moving about are necessary.

Use gravity whenever possible. Let your clothes fall from the dryer into the basket. When scooping them out, you may want to use a reacher or stick.

Laundry bags that were originally intended for washing delicate items like nylons can be used for all small pieces of clothing (socks, underwear) and thus eliminate searching in the machine.

If lifting detergent boxes is difficult, you can either have someone else pour some into a smaller container or buy the 20-pound size and scoop it out. Liquid detergents may also be more manageable.

Use a Back Preserver tool on your floor mop or push broom. Tasks can be performed with better posture and less strain to the back with this special long-handled attachment.

Try using the old-style push-on clothespins rather than pinch clothespins.

Front-loading washers are generally easier to use than top-loading washers. Raising the washer on blocks will also make laundering easier, since bending is eliminated.

Call your local grocery to find out if they deliver, and at an affordable price. Sometimes a local teenager can shop for you more economically. Also senior centers often offer shopping services.

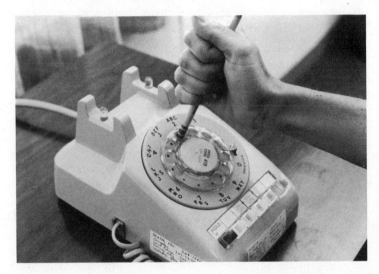

Dialing a phone may be easier with a pencil held in the palm of the hand. Also, interesting and easy-to-operate telephones (such as pushbutton models) are now widely used. Look into getting one.

Enlarged knobs are available to place on lamps as well as appliances such as washing machines (certain brands only) to increase ease of handling. Check with your washing-machine manufacturer if the controls are difficult to operate.

Use lockable casters on furniture. It will be easier to move when cleaning.

Use a box or cart to help put things away. As you move from room to room, collect things in the box and put them away when you get to the proper place.

If fitted sheets are difficult to manage, slit the last corner and fasten with a tie. Use an oven shovel to tuck in sheets.

The Touch-tronic, a device that fits into the light socket, allows you to turn lamps on and off by touching them with your fingers. It can be ordered from lighting stores.

DRIVING

When buying a car look for: doors that are easy to open and close, storage that is easy to reach, e.g. hatchback, and a seat positioner that is easy to manipulate.

Attach a loop of fabric to inside door handle to make it easier to close. (See photo of loop on refrigerator door, page 116.)

Auxiliary or wide-angle mirrors allow for increased visibility when neck movement is limited.

To make driving more comfortable and to prevent low back strain, you may want to look into Sacro Ease seats, which are especially suitable for cars. They are similar to the cooling cushion inserts used when driving during the summer, but can be bent to fit your body curvatures and support your low back.

RECREATION OR LEISURE TIME

An embroidery frame that can be attached to a table or chair will allow you to do needlework and sewing without using your hands to stabilize the article. These are available primarily through self-help aids catalogs.

If you like to play cards, try using a card holder. These can be purchased through mail-order catalogs or easily made by sawing a slit in a piece of wood.

When gardening, try sitting on a small stool instead of kneeling to weed and plant.

Gardening can be made even easier by having a planter box or raised flower beds made. This will eliminate stooping entirely, as you can sit to work at a comfortable level.

If you enjoy gardening, there is now an attachment for shovels. There is a different attachment to be used with hoes and rakes. These Back Preserver tools can easily be attached to your own equipment.

If threading a needle is difficult, self-threading needles or automatic threading machines are available through catalogs and in some sewing stores.

Afternoon exercises or sports are a really good way to break up the day. Try to set up a schedule at work where you can take an extended break to swim or exercise during the lunch hour.

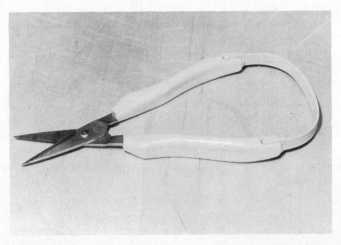

Use special clipping scissors when sewing to avoid pressure and pain on the thumb joint.

KEEPING JOINTS WARM

Use the extra-long heating pads that wrap around an arm or leg and fasten with Velcro to warm an elbow or knee.

Soak stiff, sore, or cold hands in warm water. This is especially useful to loosen them from morning stiffness. At night, warm the hands in this manner; rub hand lotion in and wear cotton gloves while sleeping.

Thermoelastic gloves are especially warming, since they are made from wool and elastic fibers. They are available in some pharmacies.

Thermoelastic products are also available for knees and elbows. A soft, thick knee sock could also be used in the same manner. Cut the sock so you have a tube approximately seven inches long and place the tube over your knee or elbow.

Use electric blankets as a lightweight cover; they are especially useful in warming the bed before you get in it.

An alternative way to stay warm during the night or when resting is to sleep inside a sleeping bag that is placed under a blanket. The bag will turn with you and prevent cold air spaces.

Use a sleeping bag, cozy-wrap, or comforter when reading in a chair.

Use a mug to drink hot tea or coffee and hold it between both hands to warm them.

Slipper socks, worn over a pair of regular socks, will help to keep feet and ankles warm.

A foot bath will not only warm your feet as they soak in the water but also can act as a massager.

Dress warmly. Use long underwear even in the spring and fall.

Place a space heater or heat lamp in your bathroom and turn it on before showering in the morning.

Stand by the radiator to warm up, or build a fire in the fireplace.

COMFORT

When sitting for long periods of time is necessary, such as when riding in a car or flying, you can relax your back muscles by doing the following. Place your forearms on your thighs, hands near the knees, and lean forward with your face as near to the knees as possible. Breathe deeply and relax in this position. Repeat several times.

Purchase a padded toilet seat, or sew a cover for it out of thick, furry material.

Pad chairs with pillows or foam cushions.

If you don't want to take a pillow with you when going out, take a sweater or jacket along to use as a cushion for hard chairs.

Recliner chairs with head supports are comfortable for many people, especially if you have neck problems.

Electric beds are no longer confined to the hospital. Home models are available that have movable back and foot sections.

Be sure that you have adequate lighting and ventilation for all activities.

If you take aspirin for pain, you may want to wake up earlier than necessary, take your aspirin, and go back to sleep until it begins to work. Keep aspirin and a glass of water at the bedside.

Splints, often made for hands and from special plastics, help to maintain proper joint alignment, prevent stress, and reduce pain. Your physician can refer you to an occupational therapist who can construct one for you.

An Ace bandage can also provide some added stability to joints, as well as serve as a reminder to use them appropriately.

MISCELLANEOUS

To control lamps, equipment, and appliances in inaccessible locations, there is a plug on the market with an on-off switch. This can plug in directly to a wall outlet or can be attached to an extension cord that can be positioned near you.

An easier, though quite expensive, method of controlling appliances and lights is with a Home Control Unit. Available through certain large department stores, this device consists of a command console and up to 16 module units for each appliance wanted. Pushing the buttons on the console will turn any appliance on or off anywhere in your house.

Use a clipboard to keep writing paper steady.

A felt-tip pen allows you to write with less pressure.

Mechanical reachers extend your reach from two to three feet, allowing you to retrieve from the floor or on high shelves.

When attending lectures, use a cassette recorder to eliminate note taking.

When shaking hands with another person, grasp the fingers or wrist of the person's hands first so that his or her thumb cannot grasp and squeeze your hand too hard.

Use a steak or paring knife at dinner since the sharper the knife, the less pressure needed. Be careful.

Make sure that the chairs you use at home are easy to get out of — if not, you may not want to get out of them often enough to move around and loosen up. Avoid soft, low chairs.

11

Getting a Good Night's Sleep

Sleep is vital for a healthy outlook toward life and important in caring for ourselves. A comfortable bed that allows ease of movement and good body support is the first requirement for a good night's sleep. This usually means a good-quality firm mattress that supports the spine and does not allow the body to sag in the middle of the bed. A bedboard, made of ⅜- or ½-inch plywood, can be placed between the mattress and the box spring to increase firmness. Bedboards can be bought commercially or constructed at home.

BEDS

Heated waterbeds or airbeds are helpful for some people with arthritis, because they support weight evenly by conforming to the body's shape. Others find these beds uncomfortable. If you are interested, try one out at a friend's home or a hotel for a few nights to decide if it is right for you.

An electric blanket, used at a low heat, is another effective way of providing heat while sleeping, especially for cool or damp nights. Or you might try an electric mattress pad. If you decide to use one or the other, be sure to read and follow the instructions carefully.

SLEEPING POSITIONS

The best sleeping position depends on which joints are involved. For most people without arthritis of the knees or hips the best position is sleeping on your side or back. In either case, it is best to use a small soft pillow to support the curvature of the neck and maintain normal neck alignment. Pillows may also be used under the knees to relieve back pain. However, care should be taken not to maintain this position continuously. If you have knee problems, check with your doctor before using a pillow under your knees even for a short period as it can cause knee contractures. In the side-laying position, a small pillow can be placed between the knees.

For people with hip or knee problems, the best sleeping position is one where the knees are straight and the hips are in a neutral position (not rotated to the sides). There are also a few do's and don'ts.

- Do try to rest on your stomach for ten to fifteen minutes a day. This will help prevent flexion contractures of the hips.

- If it does not bother you, try putting a small pillow under your ankles while sleeping on your back. (This will keep your knees straight.)

- Don't sleep with pillows under your knees, even if this is more comfortable.

For people with back problems, often a comfortable way to sleep is the side-lying position, in which you lie on your side with knees bent. In this position it can be helpful to place a pillow between the knees to alleviate stress on the hips and low back. A pillow can also be placed under the upper arm to reduce stress on the shoulder joint. But in most cases, your body will tell you the best position. There is no single right way.

If you have ankylosing spondylitis, there are some specific sleep positions that will help prevent deformity and loss of mobility of the spine. Sleep on your stomach or flat on your back. Avoid using high pillows under your head; sleep without a pillow if possible. Place a small pillow between your shoulder blades when you sleep on your back.

SLEEPING PILLS

Sedatives and sleeping pills should be used with great caution. They are often habit forming, they suppress important stages of sleep, and they may cause depression. They only rarely solve sleep problems; the medication that is taken to control sleep actually may produce a disturbed night's sleep; this is also true of alcohol. If you are using medications and decide to stop, do so gradually.

INSOMNIA

There is no known serious complication from lack of sleep. When people go without sleep long enough, they will fall asleep, so don't worry. If you can't sleep, don't lie in bed feeling guilty or bored — get up and do something you enjoy like reading a book or listening to music until you are sleepy. Remember that older persons need less sleep, so be sure your insomnia is not due to sleeping too much. There is more worry about sleeping problems than there are problems.

Still, insomnia is a problem that affects all of us at one time or another. It can be a cause of concern if it occurs frequently and involves recurrent daytime fatigue or depression. The causes of insomnia are many, some of which are feelings of anxiety or worry, pain or discomfort due to a medical condition, or an unfamiliar sleeping environment. Other contributing factors may be improper self-treatment or failure to follow the practitioner's recommended dosage or directions for medications. If your sleeping problem continues, you may want to seek a physician's advice.

Some hints for a more comfortable night's sleep include:

- Maintain a regular sleep schedule so that you go to bed and awaken at about the same time each night and morning.

- For relief of pain and inflammation at night, take aspirin or anti-inflammatory drugs as your doctor prescribes, and be sure to take the proper dose at bedtime. Painkillers should be used with great caution.

- Use some of the relaxation techniques described in this book or create one of your own that is particularly relaxing to you and will settle the day's thoughts and ease the body's tensions. (Counting backwards from 1,000 by twos or threes is especially helpful.)

- Wait until you are sleepy and your body is ready and eager to go to sleep; going to bed early to ensure a good night's sleep is often counterproductive.

- Avoid caffeine (coffee, tea, soft drinks, chocolate) for several hours before bedtime, because it can act as a stimulant.

- Moderate your alcohol intake; alcohol may cause an erratic night's sleep and restlessness. Avoid any alcohol for three or four hours before bedtime.

- Provide yourself with a comfortable environment. Your environment includes mattress, lighting, noise level, temperature, and ventilation.

- Try taking a warm bath before going to bed.

- Get as much exercise as permitted during the day.

- Don't do things that excite you just before going to sleep.

- Avoid naps if you are having problems sleeping at night.

If you do wake up with stiffness during the night, try some of the easier exercises in Chapter 7 (or small movements in the pain-free range) right in the bed to reduce discomfort and pain, allowing for a more undisturbed and restful sleep.

12

Depression and Other Problems

Depression is like waking up under a big dark cloud every day. Just when you think that you have it licked, back comes the depression, greater than ever.

One of the most frequent problems associated with arthritis is depression. Depression and pain and concerns about growing old are often part of a vicious circle. The more depressed you are, the more pain you feel; the more pain you feel, the more stressed you become. The more stressed you become, the more depressed you are.

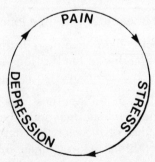

We have already discussed a number of ways to deal with pain, including heat, relaxation, and exercise. It is when you are the most depressed that you need to pay the most attention to these techniques. Continue to do these things when you are feeling well in order to maintain your good spirits. Take your medicine and do your exercises — even if you don't feel like it. But you also want to lick the depression that is making everything worse.

It is not hard to tell when you have pain. But it is not as easy to recognize when you are depressed. Just as there are many degrees of pain, so there are many different degrees of depression. If your arthritis is a significant problem, you almost certainly have or have had some problems with depression; such problems are normal. Depression is felt by everyone at some time. It is how you handle it that makes the difference. The following fourteen signs have to do with depression, and you probably have had some of them, in either mild or severe form. Learn them, because they are not the disease but the reaction to the disease, and you need to be able to cope with them.

1. Loss of interest in friends or activities. Not "being home" to friends, perhaps not even answering the doorbell.

2. Isolation. Not wanting to talk to anyone, only watching television, avoiding friends that you happen to meet on the street.

3. Difficulty sleeping, changed sleeping patterns, interrupted sleep, or sleeping more than usual. Often, going to sleep easily, but awakening and being unable to return to sleep. (It is important to remember that older people need less sleep.)

4. Loss of interest in food.

5. Loss of interest in personal care and grooming.

6. Unintentional weight change, either gain or loss, of more than ten pounds in a short period of time.

7. A general feeling of unhappiness lasting longer than six weeks.

8. Loss of interest in being held or in more intimate sex. These problems can sometimes be due to medications and they are very important, so be sure to talk them over with your doctor.

9. Suicidal thoughts. If your unhappiness has caused you to think seriously about killing yourself, get some help from your doctor, good friends, a member of the clergy, a psychologist, or a social worker. These are not things to kill yourself over, and these feelings

will pass and you will feel better. So get help and don't let a tragedy happen.

10. Frequent accidents. Watch for a pattern of increased carelessness, accidents while walking or driving, dropping things, and so forth.

11. Low self-image. A feeling of worthlessness, a negative image of your body, wondering if it is all worth it. This too will pass.

12. Frequent arguments. A tendency to blow up easily over minor matters, over things that never bothered you before.

13. Loss of energy. Feeling tired all of the time.

14. Inability to make decisions. Feeling confused and unable to concentrate.

If some of these seem familiar, you may well be depressed. There are at least eleven things that you can do to change the situation. But, being depressed, you may not feel like making the effort. Force yourself or get someone to help you into action. Find someone to talk with. Here are the eleven actions:

1. If you feel like hurting yourself or someone else, call your mental health center, doctor, suicide prevention center, a friend, clergyman, or senior center. Do not delay. Do it now. These feelings do not mean that you are crazy. Most of us feel this way at one time or another. Often, just talking with an understanding person or health professional will be enough to help you through this mood.

2. Are you taking tranquilizers? These include drugs such as Valium, Librium, reserpine, codeine, sleeping medications, and other "downers." These drugs intensify depression, and the sooner you can stop taking them, the better you will be. Your depression may well be a drug side effect. If you are not sure what you are taking or what the side effects might be, check with your doctor or pharmacist. Before discontinuing a prescription medication, always check, at least by phone, with the prescribing physician, as there may be important reasons for continuing its use or there may be withdrawal reactions.

3. Are you drinking alcohol in order to feel better? Alcohol is also a downer. There is virtually no way to escape depression unless you unload your brain from these negative influences. For most people, one or two drinks in the evening is not a problem, but if your mind is not totally free of alcohol during most of the day, you are having trouble with this drug.

4. Continue your daily activities. Get dressed every day, make your bed, get out of the house, go shopping, walk your dog. Plan and cook meals. Force yourself to do these things even if you don't feel like it.

5. Visit with friends. Call them on the phone, plan to go to the movies or on other outings. Do it.

6. Join a group. Get involved in a church group, a discussion group at a YWCA or YMCA, a senior citizen club, a community college class, a self-help class, or a senior nutrition program.

7. Make plans and carry them out. Look to the future. Plant some young trees. Look forward to your grandchildren's graduation from college even if they are in kindergarten.

8. Don't move to a new setting without first visiting for a few weeks. Moving can be a sign of withdrawal, and depression often intensifies when you are in a location away from friends and acquaintances. Your troubles may move, too.

9. Take a vacation with relatives or friends. Vacations can be as simple as a few days in a nearby city or a resort just a few miles down the road. Rather than go alone, look into trips sponsored by colleges, the American Association of Retired People, or church groups.

10. Do twenty to thirty minutes of physical exercise every day.

11. Make a list of self-rewards. Take care of yourself. You can reward yourself by reading at a set time, seeing a special play, or by anything big or small that you can look forward to.

Depression feeds on depression, so break the cycle. The success of everything else in this book depends on it. Depression is not permanent, but you can hasten its disappearance. Focus on your pride, your friends, your future goals, your positive surroundings. How you respond to depression is a self-fulfilling prophecy. When you believe that things will get better, they will.

COMMON PROBLEMS: PAIN, FEAR, FATIGUE, AND SEX

Pain

Although we have talked a lot about pain in earlier chapters, here we would like to review some basic principles and discuss the connection between pain and mood.

1. Keep active when you have pain. Get dressed in your favorite clothes; women put on makeup, men shave. Now do something. Go to work, go out shopping, go to a movie you have wanted to see. All of these activities will make you look and feel good, and will help keep your mind off the pain. If you instead stay home in your favorite old robe and stay in bed or mope around the house, you will have too much time to think about your pain and it will seem worse than it is.

2. Do your exercises. Unless you are in a "flare" and have "hot" joints, your exercises will help. Some of the pain of arthritis is due to stiff, unused muscles. Therefore, it is very important to keep your muscles in strong, supple condition. Muscle strength will also help keep your joints stable.

3. Practice relaxation exercises. Relaxed muscles and nerve endings send out fewer pain messages and thus you have less pain.

4. Don't be a martyr. Pain is individual, and it cannot be seen. Therefore, don't be afraid to tell friends and family members that you are in pain. Ask for help in carrying groceries, making beds, or mowing the lawn. Don't worry if people look at you strangely. Remember that people usually can't see your arthritis or tell that it is hurting you. A direct request for help is not being dependent; it is a direct, honest, and often necessary communication.

5. Pain is closely related to stress and depression. Thus, reducing stress and depression will also reduce pain. Sometimes people are not aware of how closely attitude and pain are related. Thus, we suggest a simple exercise. For a week, keep a pain/mood diary like the one on the next page. Each day make a mark to reflect your general pain level and mood for that day. At the end of the week, connect all the pain marks and then all the mood marks. We think that you will be able to see a close connection.

Fear

People with arthritis, especially in early stages, have many fears, particularly the fear of disability, loss of independence, or of deformity. First, you should know that most people with arthritis never have any major disability or deformity. And even if you do have a mild deformity, it will very seldom be noticed by others. We see what we expect to see, and seldom notice any but the most extreme deformities. To prove this for yourself spend a day carefully observing others for deformity or disability. You will be surprised at how many you find; it is just that usually we don't notice.

PAIN/MOOD DIARY

Each day, put a dot somewhere between "No Pain" and "Terrible Pain" to indicate your pain for that day. Do the same for your mood. After a week, connect the dots. You may be surprised to see the connections between your mood and your pain.

PAIN

	SUN.	MON.	TUES.	WED.	THURS.	FRI.	SAT.
No Pain							
Terrible pain							

MOOD

	SUN.	MON.	TUES.	WED.	THURS.	FRI.	SAT.
Feeling Great							
Feeling Awful							

Second, don't keep your fear to yourself. Fear feeds on fear and grows into depression. Talk to someone, perhaps a friend, your doctor, or a family member. Often, talking with someone is the best thing that you can do. If you don't feel comfortable talking with any of these people, you may want to call your local health department or mental health department. Seeking help with your fears is a very healthy thing to do; the reality is never as bad as you are afraid it will be.

Fatigue

There is no question about it, arthritis can be very draining of energy. This is particularly true of rheumatoid arthritis, but it can be a problem in any type of arthritis. Thus, know that fatigue is a part of the overall problem and that you are not just imagining it. Know also that fatigue can be a sign of depression, so you should consider whether the fatigue might be lessened by treating the depression.

If the fatigue is caused by your disease, then there are several things that you can do.

1. Conserve your energy (see Chapter 9).

2. Do the obvious — rest! Take a short nap once or twice a day. If this is impossible, then just relax. Try doing a relaxation exercise.

3. Fatigue, like pain and fear, cannot be seen and is not understood by most people. Therefore tell your boss, friends, and family that fatigue is one of the problems of your arthritis and that you may have to take short rests from time to time. Gain their support in allowing you to rest. Most employers are more than willing to allow a little extra rest time for good employees. You, your family, your friends, and your employer should understand that there is a difference between fatigue and being lazy.

4. Take a good long look at yourself. Will you allow yourself to rest? Many of us build our self-images around the false ideal of being indestructible — supermom, macho man, or the perfect worker. If this is you, then reassess your position. Fatigue is one of the body's major early warning systems; it is telling you to take heed. Tune into your own body and follow its directions. The ability to rest is a strength and not a weakness.

Sex

Sexuality does not cease with a diagnosis of arthritis; but the pain and burden of the disease may make the expression of our sexuality difficult. It need not be. A full, loving sex life is available to all of us.

Sexuality encompasses much more than physical intercourse; it can serve our basic needs for intimacy, for affection, approval, and acceptance. It also reinforces our individuality. Each of us expresses our sexual needs uniquely, depending on our beliefs and values and our upbringing.

Unfortunately, these beliefs can stifle our sexual pleasure. We are apt to hold on to assumptions that limit the enjoyment we will permit ourselves. "Disabled people have no desire for sex." "No one could find my body attractive." "A woman ought not to ask for sex." If we hope to appreciate and enjoy our sexuality, we must understand how these kinds of assumptions about ourselves and our loved ones can inhibit us.

For example, here is a case we have seen often: A woman has arthritis. Her husband is afraid of causing her more pain during intercourse, so he is hesitant to initiate sex. She mistakenly thinks that her husband no longer finds her attractive. At this point, the situation serves to reinforce her husband's initial fear that he causes her pain. He may begin to feel deprived or resentful and draw away from his wife emotionally. Or he may begin to have feelings of inadequacy of helplessness about himself, with the same result; he draws away from his wife. Nobody wins; everybody loses.

Clear communication is *the* tool for resolving this common impasse. Each partner must *clearly* convey his or her needs and desires to the other, or they are destined to have an unsatisfying relationship.

What do you do if arthritis pain and fatigue is a hindrance to a sexual relationship? Some ideas for coping with pain and fatigue are found earlier in this chapter. We will not address physical positioning or technique. Articles on this topic are available from your doctor or local Arthritis Foundation office. While knowledge of different love-making techniques can be valuable to someone who might otherwise be experiencing pain during intercourse, no technique or position alone will guarantee satisfaction unless there is a willingness to explore and communicate the many aspects of sexuality with one's partner.

Many of us reserve our love and trust for everyone but ourself. We insist on seeing ourselves as unlovable, and when we do, it is not surprising that others around us come to share that view. We have to work at letting go of those "unlovable" assumptions. "Who could love my body?" "I don't deserve love." "I'm being selfish." Few of us compare very well with the Madison Avenue ideal of sexual attractiveness. If we persist in trying to live up to this ideal, we are bound to remain dissatisfied. We must instead decide that we need and deserve sexual happiness *now just as we are*.

One final word: Sex can actually help the pain of arthritis. It seems that the excitement of sex stimulates our bodies to produce cortisone, adrenalin, and other chemicals that help to ease pain naturally; use this information as you see fit!

A note about partners of people with arthritis. Many husbands and wives have told us how hard it is to watch their spouse suffer with arthritis. They feel helpless and sometimes guilty that they can't in some way share in their partner's distress. It is hard to live with arthritis, even if you don't have it. We suggest that you talk these problems over with other partners of people with arthritis. You can find such folks through your doctor, arthritis classes, or your local Arthritis Foundation. The important thing is to know that you are not alone and that your feelings are normal.

13

What About Those Diets?

The area of foods, diet, and nutrition is one of special concern to many people with arthritis. People have many questions — "Will this food help my arthritis?" "Is there any food I should avoid?" "How can I lose weight?" — and reliable answers aren't always easy to find. In this chapter we will try to answer the basic questions and show how food and nutrition really fit into the picture.

WHAT IS "GOOD NUTRITION," ANYWAY?

To understand what is meant by good nutrition and what it has to do with good health, let us examine what is meant by the words *diet, nutrients,* and *nutrition.* Your diet is simply what you eat and drink each day. Nutrients are the many substances in your food that your body needs to work correctly. When we speak of nutrition, we mean your diet, the nutrients in it, and the whole process whereby the nutrients are used by your body. Good nutrition, then, means giving your body all the nutrients it needs, in the right amounts (not too much, not too little), when it needs them.

177

HOW CAN GOOD NUTRITION HELP ME?

Good nutrition helps everyone. It can help you feel fit and energetic rather than tired and weak. If you have special problems with weight or with water retention, it can help solve them. In general, good eating habits can help you feel and be as healthy and full of life as possible.

If you have arthritis, can a good diet be especially helpful? The answer is both yes and no. No special foods or diets will cure your arthritis or make it go away. However, by helping you deal with other problems (such as overweight) and helping you feel more fit, proper nutrition can help you cope better with arthritis.

WHAT NUTRIENTS DOES MY BODY NEED? WHY DO I NEED THEM?

Your body needs many nutrients (over 40 of them) to stay healthy. It is impractical to list all the nutrients and their uses, but the list below is a rough guide. Remember that the nutrients are spread throughout the foods we eat. No one food is "complete" or perfect, but many contain several nutrients.

BASIC NUTRIENT	PURPOSE
1. Water	Water is the "main ingredient" of your body. Water provides the proper environment for the processes that go on inside your body.
2. Carbohydrates	Carbohydrates are what we usually call sugars and starches. Carbohydrates are a main source of energy (calories). They serve as the main fuel for your body's activities.
3. Proteins	Proteins are needed for growth and for the maintenance and repair of your body's tissues (muscles, organs, bones, etc.). They also supply energy and calories.
4. Fats	Fats serve as a source of energy and as a source for certain vitamins. The fat in your body is a form of stored energy, like a reserve fuel supply.
5. Vitamins	Vitamins help control and regulate the various processes that go on in your body. Each vitamin has certain specific tasks and roles in the body, which do not change. Vitamins do *not* supply energy.

6. Minerals   Minerals help control and regulate certain body
                      activities. They also have a role in building and
                      repairing tissues.

7. Fiber   Fiber helps with the regulation of bowel func-
                      tion.

WHAT'S THE BEST WAY TO GET THE NUTRIENTS I NEED?

Just choose wisely which foods you eat. You might think that this is
difficult, since there are so many nutrients. But actually, it isn't hard if
you follow these guidelines.

Guideline 1.   Think of calories as a "currency," like money. Depending on your size, your age, and your physical activity you have a
certain number of calories you can "spend" each day on foods and still
maintain a good weight. (Those of us who are fairly inactive probably
have from 1500 to 2500 calories to spend each day.) With the calorie
"budget" you have, you need to include all the nutrients your body
needs.

If your calorie budget is small (as it is when you aren't very active,
or are trying to lose weight), you need to shop around for "nutrition
bargains" — foods that supply many nutrients, yet have relatively few
calories. You simply can't afford to spend calories on "luxury" foods
that don't provide many nutrients. If you do want an occasional luxury
food, or a little more freedom from bargain hunting, you need to increase the number of calories you have to spend. The best way is to
increase your physical activity.

Guideline 2.   Think of the variety in your diet as your "good nutrition insurance." It is possible to eat just a few foods and have an
adequate diet, but it is difficult. People whose diets are varied have a
better chance of getting all the nutrients they need.

The reason variety helps is that no food gives you every nutrient,
and many only give you a few. When you eat only a few foods, you may
be getting a lot (even too much) of a few nutrients and very little of the
rest. If you eat many different foods, you are probably getting moderate
amounts of many nutrients, which is better.

Guideline 3.   Think about making a few changes in your general
eating habits. Most of us would be healthier if we cut down on the salt,
fat, and sugar we eat and added more *complex carbohydrates*. Complex
carbohydrates include fruits and vegetables, plus what we usually
think of as starches (breads, cereals, grains, etc.). One benefit of these
foods is that many of them (especially fruits, vegetables, and whole-

grain products) provide fiber, which promotes proper bowel function. Refined sugars and sweets are not complex carbohydrates.

Many older adults cut back on fruits and vegetables because they feel that some of these cause constipation. Nothing is further from the truth. It is important to use these liberally in your diet.

Guideline 4.   Keep the following Consumer's Guide to Eating in mind when you purchase, prepare, and eat your meals.

Things to Remember When Using the Consumer's Guide to Eating

1. The serving sizes and number are only a basic pattern. If you are quite active, you may need to add more food. If you are very sedentary, you may need to focus on the lower-calorie foods in each group.

2. Variety is important. Don't depend on just one or two foods in each group. Experiment a little.

3. Try not to add much fat or sugar to the foods you eat, especially if you are trying to lose weight.

4. Don't eliminate the milk products. (But use nonfat or low-fat milk.) People with arthritis still need calcium, and calcium is hard to get without dairy products. (See Chapter 4.)

5. Vegetables and fruits will be more nutritious if they are cooked in only a small amount of water. Steam your vegetables instead of boiling them.

6. You don't need to buy expensive foods or "health foods" to be well nourished. There are relatively inexpensive nutritious foods in every group.

7. If you are watching your food costs, it can be helpful to cut down on the number of prepared convenience foods you eat and/or eat less meat and substitute less expensive sources of protein, such as beans, fish, cheese, or chicken which are also better for you.

8. Consider substituting other sources of protein. Many people think that they need to eat meat every day. Actually, what they need is to get enough high-quality protein each day. Protein is composed of smaller units called *amino acids*. There are nine amino acids that your body needs but cannot make. High-quality protein is protein that contains these nine amino acids in the right proportions to meet human needs.

THE CONSUMER'S GUIDE TO EATING FOR GOOD NUTRITION

Food Group	Includes	Is a Major Source of	Approximate Serving Size	Number of Servings Needed per Day
Grains and cereals	Whole grain or enriched cereals, grains (including rice), breads, rolls, pasta, etc. (not cakes, cookies, pastries, etc.)	Carbohydrate, fiber, B vitamins	1 slice bread, *or* ½ cup cooked cereal or grains, *or* 1 oz. dry cereal (about ¾–1 cup for many cereals)	4 or more per day
Vegetables and fruits	All vegetables and fruits (pure juices may be used, but should not entirely replace whole foods) (avocados and olives are high in fat, high in calories)	Carbohydrate, fiber, iron, vitamin A, vitamin C	½ cup or 1 medium-size piece of fruit *Vitamin C* rich foods: citrus fruits, canteloupe, tomatoes, strawberries, raw cabbage, potatoes, leafy green vegetables *Vitamin A* rich foods: dark green vegetables (broccoli, kale, chard, spinach, etc.), deep yellow or orange fruits and vegetables (pumpkin, carrots, squash, apricots, sweet potatoes, etc.)	4 or more per day, including: 1 vitamin C food per day; 1 vitamin A food several times a week
Milk products	Milk (low-fat or skim preferred), cheeses (including cottage cheese), yogurt (plain has less sugar), ice cream (for occasional use) (not butter, cream, cream cheese; these are high in fat, relatively low in other nutrients)	Protein, calcium and phosphorus (minerals), riboflavin (a vitamin)	1 cup milk or yogurt, *or* 1–1½ oz. cheese, *or* 1/3 cup nonfat dry milk powder, *or* 1–1½ cups cottage cheese	2 or more per day; postmenopausal women should consider 4 a day
Meats	Meat (preferably lean, trimmed of fat), poultry, fish, eggs, nuts (including peanut butter), legumes (dried beans and peas)	Protein, iron, B vitamins	3 oz. (excluding the bone) of cooked meat, fish, or poultry, *or* 2 eggs, *or* 4 tablespoons of peanut butter, *or* 1 cup dried beans or other meat substitute prepared appropriately	2 or more per day
Other foods	Fats, oils, sugar, sweets, alcohol	These foods supply few nutrients	Limit the amount eaten When using fats try to use only those that are soft or liquid at room temperature. These fats are lower in cholesterol.	You probably get more than enough without adding anything

Meat, milk, and eggs all provide high-quality protein. Most vegetables and grains don't provide high-quality protein when eaten by themselves. This is because the proportions of amino acids in plant proteins often don't match the proportions that people need. However, if several plant foods are combined properly in a meal, the body can get high-quality protein, because one food's amino acids "fill in the gaps" the other leaves.

Legumes and grains are a good example of two vegetable products that "match" or complement each other very well. Legumes (dried beans and peas) are relatively low in two amino acids that grains have plenty of, and grains are low in two amino acids that legumes can provide.

The following ten combinations of plant products will provide good, usable protein.

beans and rice	rice, soybeans, and wheat
beans and corn	peanuts, wheat, and milk
beans and wheat	peanuts, soybeans, and sesame
beans and sesame	peanuts and sunflower seeds
rice and sesame	greens and rice

When using rice make sure it is brown rice, wild rice, or converted rice, all of which have more vitamins and minerals than polished white rice.

HOW ABOUT VITAMIN AND MINERAL SUPPLEMENTS? ARE THEY A GOOD WAY TO MAKE SURE I GET THE NUTRIENTS I NEED?

Depending on supplements is not a good idea. The five reasons for this are listed below. The same comments usually apply to cereals and other foods that are "fortified" with several vitamins and minerals.

1. Your body needs many nutrients, not just a few. When you take a supplement, you get only a few of the essential nutrients. The rest are ignored.

2. Supplements can give people a false sense of nutritional security. Some people feel that once they take their pill (or pills) they are "okay" for the day. So they don't think about the nutritive value of the foods they eat. They may end up with worse nutrition than they would have had if they hadn't taken the supplement.

3. Supplements tend to be expensive. Most people would be better off spending more on healthy foods, where money buys many nu-

trients, than on special supplements, where several dollars may buy only a few nutrients.

4. It is possible to get "too much of a good thing." Some vitamins and minerals build up in the body and are hard to get rid of. If people take in too much of these nutrients, health problems can result. Talk with your doctor before taking "megavitamins."

5. We may not know about all the nutrients humans need yet. If you depend on supplements, you get only the nutrients that the manufacturer, with current knowledge, chooses to add. But if you depend on a variety of good foods, you get all the "extras" nature adds. This may be much better.

6. If you are a post-menopausal woman, you may need a supplement. In this case, taking calcium to prevent osteoporosis may be a good idea. See Chapter 4 for more details.

HOW CAN I USE NUTRITION AND FOODS TO HELP WITH MY ARTHRITIS?

Unless you have gout, there are no specific foods or diets that will cure or directly treat your arthritis. However, there are several things that can help you. Controlling your weight and coordinating your meals with your medications can be helpful. If so advised by your physician, restricting your salt intake may be useful. Finally, you can help yourself by learning how to critically judge "diet cures" for arthritis, so that you don't fall into any traps.

Controlling Your Weight

If you are overweight, you are putting extra loads and stress on your weight-bearing joints. This makes little sense if you have arthritis — it may make the pain or inflammation worse. Reducing your weight makes more sense — it will ease the strain, lessen the pain, improve your agility, and make you both look and feel better.

Losing weight can be a difficult task, but it is possible. If you need to reduce, perhaps this information will make the job easier.

Calories are essentially a measure of the fuel value of foods. They tell you how much work your body can do with the energy it gets when you eat a particular food. People get overweight and overfat if they eat more calories than their body needs for its activities. To lose weight and fat, they need to consume fewer calories than they use up. If, over a period of time, a person eats 3500 calories less than he or she needs, he or she will lose one pound.

There are no hard and fast rules about how to lose weight success-fully, but following these steps may be helpful.

Step 1: Decide to lose weight and to change your eating habits. People are rarely successful in achieving permanent weight loss if they lack strong commitment to the idea. Check with your doctor to make sure that he or she recommends that you lose weight.

Step 2: Before you start, think about why you are overweight. Doing this may give you some clues about things you can do to help yourself. For example:

• Some people eat too much because cooking is one of their hobbies. They enjoy eating a great deal. For them, it may help to prepare less food and to serve smaller portions.

• Some people are overweight because they (over)eat when they get into a certain mood. They eat when they get depressed, bored, or nervous. In these cases, it may be important for people to find and plan something else to do, such as call a friend, take a warm bath, or take a walk.

• Some people eat large amounts of food almost unconsciously while they do other things. For them it is important to focus on the foods they eat, to eat slowly, and not to do anything else while they eat.

• Some people are overweight not because they eat so much more than anyone else but because they aren't as active. In this situation, you should try to increase your physical activity; and you also should accept the fact that you may regularly need to eat much less than others if you want to have a normal, moderate weight.

It may be easier for you to analyze your habits if you write down everything you eat for several days on a record like the one on the next page.

Step 3: Reduce your consumption of the "luxury" foods — high-calorie foods with little nutritive value. In general, these are the foods that are not mentioned as part of the four basic groups in the Consumer's Guide to Eating.

Step 4: Use the basic foods that are lower in fat and sugar content wherever possible. Eat leaner meats, use low-fat

DAY AND TIME	WHAT I ATE	HOW MUCH I ATE	WHERE I ATE	WHAT MOOD I WAS IN	WHAT I WAS DOING BESIDES EATING

or skim milks and cheeses. Avoid fruits canned in heavy syrup.

If necessary, eat smaller portions of the basic foods, but do not eliminate any food group. Many "low-carbohydrate" diets exclude breads and cereals as well as milk and dairy products. Do not use "crash" diets. They deprive your body of many of the nutrients it needs to be healthy, and rarely result in any long-term weight loss.

Step 5: Aim to lose weight gradually. A rate of no more than one or two pounds lost per week is best for most people. (Beware of diets that promise large, quick weight losses. With some of them, including low-carbohydrate diets, you will lose weight rapidly, but much of the loss will be water. The water will be regained quickly after you go off the diet. The aim is to lose fat, not water, so don't be deceived.)

Step 6: Don't be upset if your weight doesn't drop dramatically during the first week or if it reaches a plateau for a few weeks. When you diet, your body doesn't just burn up fat — it goes through many changes. Some of the adjustments it makes may involve changing the amount of water in your body temporarily, and this can affect your weight. But as long as you are eating less than you use up, you will be losing fat. The loss will eventually show up on the scale. If it doesn't, you are still eating too much for you. A further decrease in amount and an increase in discipline are needed.

Step 7:   Become more active. The notion of becoming more active may not sound so appealing to some people who think: "I'm too tired to do anything after a hard day at the office," "I'm getting enough exercise running around the office," or "I'm getting enough exercise doing the housework." However, it has been shown that exercise helps people develop more stamina and get tired less easily. In other words, exercise doesn't wear you down but peps you up.

People with arthritis may have a particularly difficult time working up to an exercise program — "I'm in too much pain to do any physical activity." However, increased physical activity leads to better health, and being in good health means being better able to deal with the problems caused by arthritis:

1. Losing weight means less weight your joints have to support.
2. Firm, toned muscles provide stronger support for your joints.

You can minimize the stress of exercise by choosing a program that uses the painful joint the least, but still provides a good workout.

Some additional comments on losing weight:

1. Eat only when hungry. Usually, this means to eat only at mealtimes.

2. Eat slowly. When you eat slowly, you give your body time to signal you that you've eaten enough. If you eat rapidly, your body can't respond in time. By the time it tells you to stop, you've probably eaten too much.

3. Try eating three or even four meals rather than one or two relatively large meals. This tends to help people eat less and feel more satisfied.

4. Special "dietetic" foods are not necessary. They are generally expensive and are not necessarily nutritious.

5. Try to avoid foods that contain a lot of fat or sugar and few nutrients. Sometimes you can recognize these foods because they are greasy, "rich," or very sweet. Some specific examples are:

   • sugar and sweets, cakes and cookies

   • butter, margarine, cream

   • gravies, sauces, dressing

   • fried foods

   • soft drinks, alcoholic beverages

6. Substitute low-calorie foods for your usual snacks and desserts. Some possibilities:

   • vegetable soups (except cream soups)

   • fruits (raw or canned in their own juice)

   • raw vegetables, such as celery, carrots, and cauliflower

   • coffee or tea (plain)

7. Remember that no single food is necessarily "fattening" or "slimming." Since all foods have calories, eating too much of any food can make you gain weight. Moderation in your total intake is the key.

Choosing a Diet

Most people associate losing weight with going on a diet. Perhaps you've tried going on a diet which didn't work out. Think about the diets that you've tried.

   1. **Did it require you to eat only certain foods?**

   • all-protein diet

   • cut-out-the-carbohydrates (potatoes, bread) diet

   • only-cottage-cheese-celery-and-yogurt diet

   There are problems with this type of approach to losing weight. By prohibiting yourself from eating certain foods or limiting yourself to a small range of foods, you may not be getting the nutrients that food provides. These diets are in a category of "fad diets." Fads are fashionable items in our society that don't last very long. If a diet doesn't last very long, it probably wasn't very effective. These diets often make spectacular claims such as "lose ten pounds in just three days!" Remember, the first stage of weight loss is water loss. So, those ten pounds are just fluid loss without getting to the "fat of the matter." A pound or two a week is a good goal. Plan for the long term.

2. **Did your diet help change your eating behavior?**   Denying yourself food you enjoy and eating food you don't particularly like is not an effective long-term strategy for keeping the weight off. So you struggled through four months of nothing but cottage cheese and celery to lose 60 pounds. Great! Now what? You don't expect to live solely on cottage cheese and celery for the rest of your life. After you lose the weight you wanted to, you'll start eating other things again; you'll go back to the same eating habits that made you gain all that weight in the first place. Nothing's changed; already you're setting yourself up for another diet.

Fad diets in some ways set you up for failure. If you force yourself to eat something you don't like, who can blame you if you stick to it for only a week. If the diet regimen doesn't last a week, it surely won't help you long term.

Changing your eating habits and becoming more active not only help in getting the weight off but are necessary to keep the weight off. This is easier said than done. Many people need help in maintaining weight loss. There are many excellent groups and classes. Look for a weight-loss program that:

1. Emphasizes the importance of good nutrition and the use of a wide variety of foods.

2. Gives you support in the form of ongoing meetings and long-term follow-up.

3. Emphasizes changes in eating patterns.

Coordinating Meals and Medications

Many of the drugs used for arthritis have some relationship to food intake and meals. Some of the drugs are best absorbed on an empty stomach. Others may cause stomach problems unless you take them with meals. When you get a new medication, check with your doctor or read Chapter 14 in this book to see whether you should take it with meals. Remember that if your physician asks you to take the drug "with every meal," he or she is probably assuming that you eat three meals a day. If you don't, be sure to tell the doctor so that any necessary adjustments can be made.

Aspirin is one example of a drug that should be taken with meals and with lots of fluids. Doing this helps prevent stomach irritation and upset.

Limiting Your Salt Intake

Salt (sodium chloride) plays many important roles in our bodies. We need sodium for our muscles and nerves to work properly. Sodium can attract and hold water, so we use it to keep the right amount of water in our bodies.

Some people, however, have too much water in their bodies. This can happen when people have high blood pressure. It can also happen when people take certain drugs, including some of those used with arthritis. In such cases, a physician may prescribe a low-sodium diet to help solve the problem.

It you have been asked to limit the amount of sodium in your diet, the following guidelines should be helpful.

1. Reduce the amount of table salt in your food.

   • Reduce the amount of salt used in cooking.

   • Don't use the salt shaker at the table.

   • Remember that many foods already have salt added when you buy them. Read the labels.

2. Remember that other substances besides salt contain sodium.

   • Become a label reader; look for the word *sodium*. *Sodium benzoate, sodium bicarbonate* (baking soda), and *monosodium glutamate* are examples of ingredients you may find.

3. The following foods generally contain a great deal of sodium and should be avoided.

   • processed, cured, smoked, and canned meats

   • salty popcorn, pretzels, crackers, nuts, potato chips, and so on

   • canned soups, bouillon

   • pickles, sauerkraut, and other foods treated with a brine

   • some condiments, catsup, and spicy sauces (read the label)

Avoiding Constipation

Unfortunately constipation is a problem for many people with arthritis. There are several reasons for this. Because of arthritis many people are not as physically active as they once were. In addition, some of the arthritis medications tend to be constipating. Finally, many people do not eat all the fruits and vegetables they should or they limit their fluid intake. The following are hints for preventing and dealing with constipation.

1. **Pay attention to your body's signals.**   If you have to go to the bathroom, go. Mother Nature developed that warning signal for a reason — to prevent discomfort and possible embarrassment at a later time. Also, paying heed to this warning will help your body develop an internal bowel movement schedule.

2. **Take your time in the bathroom.**

- Take deep breaths to relax the muscles.

- Tuck in the bellybutton and raise one leg to your chest.

- Take something to read; put a radio in your bathroom.

- Don't strain.

3. **Don't overuse laxatives.**   Overuse of laxatives makes the intestines "lazy" and dependent on the help of the laxatives. When your colon has to work without that aid, you may find that it can't move the material as well and constipation may result. When this happens, you'll think something's wrong and start using laxatives again. In fact, you just need to give your system a break from the laxatives.

4. **Manage your stress level.**   This can be done in a number of different ways, including with the relaxation techniques you learned in Chapter 8. Organize your work schedule to minimize your efforts and maximize your strength (doing all the upstairs work at one time, all the downstairs work at one time). Take rest periods.

5. **Eat slowly.**   Mealtime should be one of your rest periods. When you eat, concentrate on eating; don't think about other things that have to be done. Sit down, enjoy your meal. *Chew slowly.* The more you chew, the less work your stomach and intestines have to do. This all adds to better digestion. Also, eating slowly is part of a routine for people trying to lose weight.

6. **Drink enough water.**   Water adds bulk to the material in your colon and keeps it soft; this helps in moving the material along smoothly. The recommended amount to drink is eight cups per day.

7. **Exercise.**   Keeping physically active helps your waste elimination system work efficiently.

8. **Drink warm prune juice; include fiber in your diet.**   Diet fiber is that part of fruits, vegetables, and whole grain that the body cannot use and doesn't digest. Diet fiber acts as nature's laxative by retaining water so the stools are softer and easier to expel and making the stools bulkier so as to signal the colon to keep things moving. Aside from preventing constipation, fiber is believed to help prevent cancer of the colon. By increasing the speed in which the feces pass through the colon, it is thought that cancer causing substances have less time to be in the colon to do harm. Five to six grams of fiber per day is recommended for adults. You can obtain this by eating some vegetables or fresh fruits daily and by switching from white to whole wheat breads.

TABLE OF FIBER SOURCES*

Food	Fiber in 1/2 cup (grams)
All-Bran	11.5
Rolled oats, uncooked	4.5
Parsnips (cooked)	4.0
Lentils (cooked)	4.0
Corn kernels	3.2
Apple	3.1
Potatoes (cooked)	2.3
Carrots (raw)	2.0
Kidney beans (cooked)	1.8
Celery (raw)	1.5

*Food for Health: The Stanford Guide to Eating Well (Stanford, Calif.: Stanford Heart Disease Prevention Program, 1982, p. 34.)

Here are some hints for obtaining more fiber in your diet:

1. Eat an orange instead of drinking orange juice.

2. Snack on fruits, nuts, and vegetables instead of junk food. Not only will this help with constipation but also will help in keeping off extra pounds. Nuts especially are great laxatives, but watch out for their calories.

3. Eat a hot bowl of cereal for breakfast. (This fiber source may be less irritating to your system than dry bran.)

4. If you have to use a laxative, use Metamucil, a natural laxative which adds bulk. When you use antacids, avoid products that have

calcium; instead choose products such as Maalox and Milk of Magnesia that are nonconstipating.

5. Peel and cut up a grapefruit, eating it like an orange.

Evaluating Diets and "Cures" for Arthritis — How to Keep from Getting Trapped

We have already mentioned that there are no known nutritional cures for arthritis. No specific foods or nutrients make arthritis better or worse, except in the case of gout. Yet, diet "cures" for arthritis appear regularly in magazines and books, and many people are interested. At the Arthritis Center we have studied the effects of diets; those who follow these fad diets do not feel any better than those who do not.

If you are interested in learning how to read articles and books on "miracle" cures so that you can judge things for yourself and not get "trapped" into unhealthy practices, this final section is for you.

Steps to Follow in Evaluating a Report of a "Cure"

Step 1: Get a copy of the book or article in which the originator of the diet explains the diet and the "proof" of its effectiveness.

Step 2: Read the article, focusing on the evidence or "proof." Figure out what kind of evidence the author has. Does he or she try to persuade you with anecdotes — short stories of what happened to individual patients? Or does he or she present the results of scientific studies ("clinical trials")?

Step 3: Evaluate the evidence by asking yourself the following questions.

Questions for Anecdotes (Case Reports)

1. Get the facts.

   a. Who was involved?

   b. What was the treatment?

   c. What was the result? Were there any side effects from the treatment?

   d. What claims did the author make, based on this result?

2. Think about the facts, asking yourself:

    a. Could anything else have caused the claimed results?
        - Was anything besides the diet changed (medications, exercise)?
        - Could the change be a result of a psychological effect — "positive thinking" on the part of the patient?
        - Could it have been a coincidence? Arthritis pain tends to come and go.

        People often try new cures when they have the most pain, then improve and think the cure works, when it really does nothing. Usually, the improvements actually come about because the arthritis is at the "peak" of the pain cycle when he or she tries the "cure." The arthritis would improve with or without the "cure," simply because the arthritis was going into remission anyway.

    b. Were the patients different from other arthritics or from you in any important ways?

    c. If the author presents several anecdotes as evidence, are there any patterns, other than that the patient followed the diet and improved? In one popular book that deals with nutrition and arthritis, the author presents a number of cases in which patients followed a specific diet and improved. But if one looks closely, there is another pattern — many of the patients also lost considerable amounts of weight. This sort of thing should make you suspect that maybe it isn't the specific diet but rather the weight loss that caused the improvement.

Questions for Clinical Trials (Studies)

When you read anecdotes, you will probably find that it is difficult to answer the questions suggested above. Observations of single "cases" simply do not give enough information to tell whether treatments really work. That is the reason clinical trials are done — they help us sort out the effects of the treatment from psychological effects, coincidence, and other such things.

A clinical trial is an experiment in which one group of people gets a treatment ("Treatment X"), a similar group gets no treatment or a "traditional" treatment, and the results for the two groups are compared. If the group with the new treatment does better than the other group (the "control" group), the conclusion is that the new treatment helps. But if roughly the same proportion of people get better in both groups, the conclusion is that the new treatment has no effect or at least no more effect than the old treatment.

The following diagram may make the situation clearer. In this case, the conclusion is that Treatment X does not help, because the same number of people got better in both groups. But notice that if the researcher had only looked at the people getting Treatment X (as in case reports), he or she would probably have made the opposite (wrong) conclusion, that the treatment does help.

100 PEOPLE WITH ARTHRITIS

50 get Treatment X   50 get no treatment

30 improve   30 improve
20 don't improve   20 don't improve

Here are some questions to ask yourself when people present results from clinical studies.

1. Were the two groups of people really similar? If they were not, the differences between them might have confused the study, making it give deceptive results. For example, if the group receiving no treatment has more severe arthritis, its members may not improve as much as members of the other group, whose problems are less severe. If this happens, the study may make it seem that Treatment X works better than no treatment, even though it really makes no difference. (Some things that may need to be similar in compared groups are age, sex, weight, exercise and activity patterns, and severity and type of arthritis.)

2. Were the researchers looking for a specific result? If they really wanted to prove that one group did better than the other, it may have biased them, affecting the way they saw things. ("You see what you want to see" can apply to research too, if you're not careful.)

3. Is the study published anywhere in a recent scientific journal? Editors of such magazines usually check and screen articles quite thoroughly. If a study is not published, it may mean that there are real flaws in the procedures used.

   Step 4: If you are still not sure whether you should try the diet (after you evaluate the evidence), try to contact your doctor or a nutritionist to get advice.

Step 5: If you are unable to contact anyone, or if you still think
that the diet may be good, ask yourself these questions:

1. Does the diet eliminate any of the basic foods or nutrients? (If so,
   you may well be harming your health if you follow it.)

2. Does the diet stress only a few foods, so that you will have few
   calories left to "spend" on the basic foods? (Again, if it does, you
   may be harming your health.)

3. Do the foods or supplements cost more than you can afford? (If so,
   following the diet may force you to cut back on other essentials,
   which is not good.)

4. Are you willing to put up with the trouble and expense involved,
   knowing that the chances are good that it won't be a cure?

If you answer no to the first three questions and yes to the last, it
probably won't harm you to try the diet and see if it works for you.
Remember, though, that even if it does seem to work for you, it may not
work for someone else.

14

The Drug Scene
Know About the Medications That Help Arthritis

Knowing about your drugs is not easy. No drug is simple and a full explanation from your doctor invariably takes a lot of time. Unfortunately, that time is not always available. The interview with your doctor is an intensive experience. All too frequently discussion of the prescribed treatment serves as a quick end to the encounter. Too little time is spent on this important subject. Here, the discussions you have been having with your physician are repeated. Read the ones you need. Reread those you forget.

DRUGS TO REDUCE INFLAMMATION

Many important arthritis medicines reduce inflammation, and you have to know a little bit about this concept. Inflammation is part of the normal healing process. The body increases blood flow and sends inflammatory cells to repair wounded tissues and to kill bacterial invaders. The inflammation causes the area to be warm, red, tender, and often swollen. To understand the potential problems of drugs that reduce inflammation, it is important to recognize that inflammation is a normal process.

In rheumatoid arthritis the inflammation causes damage and thus suppression of the inflammation can be helpful in treatment. In osteoarthritis there is little inflammation or the inflammation may be necessary for the healing process. So you don't always want an anti-inflammatory drug just because you have arthritis — in rheumatoid arthritis, yes; in osteoarthritis, probably no.

Aspirin is one of the most important drugs for arthritis. Not only is it useful itself, but it also serves as a model for understanding the benefits and problems of medical treatments for arthritis.

Aspirin is the most frequently used drug in the world and the most misunderstood. It is among the safest drugs currently used in the United States, yet we constantly hear of its dangers. It has become downgraded by its very familiarity. Sometimes it is used as a symbol of a physician's neglect: "Take two aspirin and call me in the morning." Yet it is said to be so powerful that today the FDA would not license it if it were a new drug. The scare press reports the hazards of bleeding from the stomach or of liver damage. The same press reports the next day that aspirin may prevent heart attacks by thinning the blood. These contradictions dominate our daily encounters with aspirin.

If used properly, aspirin is a marvelous drug for many kinds of arthritis. If not used correctly, it can lead to real frustration. Read the next several paragraphs carefully; they illustrate things you need to know about aspirin specifically, but also illustrate general principles you need to know about all arthritis medications.

What You Need to Know
About Anti-Inflammatory Medications

1. **You must know the difference between the terms *analgesic* and *anti-inflammatory*.** Analgesic means "pain-killing." Anti-inflammatory means that the redness and swelling are reduced. Aspirin provides minor pain relief and is helpful for headaches, sunburn, or other familiar problems. But it can be a major anti-inflammatory agent and can actually decrease the swelling and tissue damage in rheumatoid arthritis.

With aspirin the dosage is the difference. The pain-killing effects of aspirin are best after 2 tablets (10 grains). If you take more aspirin, you do not really get any more pain relief. You can repeat this analgesic (pain-killing) dose every 4 hours because it tends to wear off in about that time. In contrast, the anti-inflammatory activity requires high and continuous levels of aspirin in the blood. A person must take 12 to 24 tablets (5 grains each) each day and the process must be continued for 3 to 4 weeks to obtain the full effect.

2. **You need to know the difference between allergy and side effects.**   People often maintain that they cannot tolerate a drug because of problems they have had with it in the past. When the doctor asks what drugs you are allergic to, you may mention such drugs because of the problems you have had. Most of the time, you have had a side effect from the drug, not an allergy.

Allergy is relatively rare; side effects are common. Only a few people get an allergy, but everyone experiences side effects if they get enough of a drug. There are different symptoms. A skin rash, wheezing in the lungs, or a runny nose generally mean allergy. Nausea, abdominal pain, ringing in the ears, and headache usually mean side effects. If you have an allergy, that is a good reason to avoid that drug in the future. If you have side effects to a drug, usually it means that you need one or another trick to get your body to tolerate the drug better, or perhaps just a little lower dose.

These considerations are particularly important with aspirin. The treatment range is just below the level that gives side effects. So most patients receiving aspirin for anti-inflammatory purposes will have some ringing in the ears or some nausea. This is just a signal to slow down a little bit and to establish what dose is exactly the correct one for you. If you do not know this principle, you are going to give up too soon on a superb drug, and you will not get better.

3. **You also need to know about drug absorption and drug interactions.**   Food delays the absorption of a medicine into your body. With some drugs the presence of food in your stomach will totally prevent the absorption of the medication. But food also protects the stomach lining and can make taking a drug more comfortable. Thus, although food may decrease the effectiveness of a medication, it also may decrease certain side effects by protecting the stomach. By and large, antacids (Maalox, Mylantin, Gelusil) act just about the same as food; they decrease absorption but protect the stomach.

Some medications are coated to protect the stomach; the coating is designed to dissolve after the tablet has passed through the stomach into the small bowel. These coatings work for some people. On occasion, the coating never dissolves and the person derives no benefit whatsoever from the drug; it passes unaltered into the toilet. On other occasions the coating doesn't last long enough and nausea is encountered anyway.

Drugs are chemicals. Interactions between two drugs (two chemicals) are extremely common. Aspirin blocks absorption from the stomach of some of the newer anti-inflammatory agents discussed in the next section. By and large, the fewer medicines you take at one time, the more predictable your response to treatment will be. Most reactions having to do with absorption or interactions with other drugs are not perfectly predictable. You may have them or you may not. The treatment for your arthritis will ultimately be unique to you. You may need to discover by trial and error some of the reactions of your own body. To figure things out, it helps if you know the final general point.

4. **You should know about dosage equivalents, generic names, and product differences.** Aspirin is huckstered more than any other drug. It is found in the drugstore in several hundred different formulations. It is "the drug doctors recommend most." Manufacturers compete to find tiny areas of difference between products that can be exploited by advertising campaigns. There are "arthritis extra-strength" aspirins, buffered aspirins, and coated aspirins. There is aspirin with extra ingredients, such as caffeine or phenacetin. There is aspirin in cold formulations with antihistamines or other compounds. There is aspirin that is advertised for its purity.

Aspirin

Color: white

A standard aspirin tablet is five grains, USP (*United States Pharmacopoeia* — the legal standard for drug strength and purity). This is 325 milligrams (mg) and the amount of drug is accurate to government standards. You always pay more for a brand-name formulation. For arthritis, do not buy aspirin that is compounded with any drugs other than possibly an antacid (Bufferin, Ascriptin). Even then, you may find it less expensive to take aspirin with an antacid such as Maalox rather than to buy buffered aspirin. You do not want the caffeine, the phenacetin, or the antihistamine ingredients. Do not use a coated aspirin (Ecotrin, Enseals) unless you have stomach problems with regular aspirin. They are more expensive and you may not get as good absorption from your stomach. All of the USP aspirins are pure enough for your use. If your body can tell a difference, stay with a product that seems to work for you. Otherwise, buy the cheapest USP aspirin that you can find. If it smells like vinegar when you open the bottle, it is too old and you should throw it out. If you have problems with the new child-proof caps, ask your pharmacist for a regular top.

The advice that follows is general advice. If your doctor's advice differs, listen to your doctor. He or she is most familiar with your specific needs. The doses and precautions listed are those known at the time of this writing and are subject to changes your doctor may know about. But if you receive advice that doesn't make sense according to the principles outlined in this section, don't hesitate to ask questions or get another opinion.

ACETYLSALICYLIC ACID (ASPIRIN)
Indications

Pain relief for osteoarthritis and local conditions such as bursitis. Anti-inflammatory agent for rheumatoid arthritis.

Dosage

For pain, two 5-grain tablets (10 grains) every four hours as needed. For anti-inflammatory action, three to four tablets, four to six times daily (with medical supervision if these doses are continued for longer than one week). The time to maximum effect is 30 minutes to one hour for pain and one to six weeks for the anti-inflammatory action.

Side Effects

Common effects include nausea, vomiting, ringing in the ears, and decreased hearing. Each of these is reversible within a few hours if the drug dosage is decreased. Allergic reactions are rare but include development of nasal polyps and wheezing. Prolonged nausea or vomiting that persists after the drug is stopped for a few days suggest the possibility of a stomach ulcer caused by the irritation of the aspirin. With an overdose of aspirin, there is very rapid and heavy breathing, and there can even be unconsciousness and coma. Be sure to keep your aspirin (and all medications) out of reach of children or visiting grandchildren.

Aspirin has some predictable effects that occur in just about everyone. Blood loss through the bowel occurs in almost all persons who take aspirin, because the blood clotting function is altered, the stomach is irritated, and aspirin acts as a minor blood-thinning agent. Up to 10 percent of those taking high doses of aspirin will have some abnormalities in the function of the liver; although these are seldom noticed by the person taking aspirin, they can be identified by blood tests. Since serious liver damage does not occur, routine blood tests to check for this complication are not required.

Special Hints

If you note ringing in the ears or a decrease in your hearing, then decrease the dose of aspirin. Your dose is just a little bit too high for the best result. If you notice nausea, an upset stomach, or vomiting, there are a variety of things you can do. First, try spreading out the dose with more frequent use of smaller numbers of pills. Perhaps instead of taking four tablets four times a day, you might take three tablets five or six times a day. Second, try taking the aspirin after meals or after an antacid, which will coat the stomach and provide some protection. Third, you can change brands and see if the nausea is related to the particular brand of aspirin you were using. Fourth, you can try coated aspirin. These are absorbed variably, but are often effective in protecting the stomach and decreasing nausea. Ecotrin is the best absorbed, and Enseals is next best. Probably other brands of coated preparations should be avoided, since some of them are absorbed by very few people.

Ecotrin
5 gr

Color: orange

Finally, although it is a nuisance, you can get good relief from the nausea by taking a suspension of aspirin rather than the tablet. Put the aspirin in a half glass of water and swirl it until the aspirin particles are suspended in the water. Fill another glass half full of water, drink the suspended aspirin, and wash it down with the other glass of water. This is an effective and inexpensive way to avoid nausea once you get used to the taste.

Keep track of your aspirin and always tell your doctor exactly how much you are taking. Aspirin is so familiar that sometimes we forget that we are taking a drug. Be as careful with aspirin as you would be with any drug. In particular, you may want to ask your doctor about interactions with the newer anti-inflammatory agents, with probenecid, or with blood-thinning agents, if you are taking those drugs. Pay special attention to your stomach. So many drugs cause irritation to the stomach lining that you run the risk of adding insult to injury. Two drugs that irritate the stomach lining may be more than twice as dangerous; again, the fewer medications at one time the better. Every time you talk to a doctor about drugs, be sure to describe all the drugs you are taking, not just your arthritis drugs. It is a good idea to keep a list of all the drugs you take and have it ready to show any doctor you visit, including your dentist.

TRILISATE (CHOLINE MAGNESIUM TRISALICYLATE)

Trilisate
500mg

Color: pale orange

Purpose

To relieve pain; to reduce inflammation.

Indications

For mild pain relief of cartilage degeneration, local conditions. Also an anti-inflammatory agent for synovitis, attachment arthritis.

Dosage

For pain, one or two tablets every twelve hours. Tablets are 500 mg in size. For anti-inflammatory activity, two to three tablets each twelve hours. Each Trilisate tablet is equivalent in salicylate content to ten grains of aspirin (two usual-sized aspirin tablets). Occasionally higher doses may be needed. The maximum effect is reached in two hours for pain effects; one to six weeks are required for anti-inflammatory action to take full effect.

Side Effects

Common effects include nausea, vomiting, ringing in the ears, and decreased hearing. Each of these is reversible within a few hours if the drug dosage is decreased. Allergic reactions are rare but potentially include development of nasal polyps and wheezing. With an overdose of salicylate, there can be very rapid and heavy breathing, and even unconsciousness and coma.

Trilisate has been urged as a drug of choice in arthritis because it is much less toxic to the stomach than is aspirin. Additionally, there is less effect upon the platelets, so there is less chance of a bleeding problem. The blood salicylate level rises more slowly and lasts longer; hence, the drug does not have to be taken as often as aspirin.

But a controversy has arisen because some physicians do not

believe that the anti-inflammatory activity of Trilisate is nearly as good as that of aspirin. Other physicians believe that the effects are identical. So, it seems clear that Trilisate is less toxic than ordinary aspirin, but it is not clear that it is as effective a drug. It finds particular use in patients who have had problems with stomach upset from ordinary aspirin. Trilisate does require a prescription; it is not clear why a prescription should be required for this drug any more than for regular aspirin.

Special Hints

If you note ringing in the ears or a decrease in your hearing, decrease the dose of Trilisate; it is just a little bit too high for the best results. Keep track of your Trilisate intake, and always tell the doctor exactly how much you are taking. It is possible that there may be drug interference between Trilisate and the nonsteroidal anti-inflammatory agents discussed in the following pages, so you will usually not want to take them at the same time.

Other Anti-inflammatory Agents That Are Not Steroids

Aspirin is a *nonsteroidal anti-inflammatory agent* (NSAIA). That is, it is not a corticosteroid (like prednisone), and it is an anti-inflammatory agent because it fights inflammation. But some of the disadvantages of aspirin have been noted above. In anti-inflammatory doses, side effects such as nausea, vomiting, and ringing in the ears are common. Some persons can't tolerate these side effects. Others, either ill-advised or not persistent, don't really try. Aspirin requires many tablets and regular attention to the medication schedule. So, a class of "aspirin substitutes," given the cumbersome name of nonsteroidal anti-inflammatory agents, has been developed. In common medical usage, aspirin is not included in this group. To further simplify, we use the term *anti-inflammatory drugs* in this book. In the over-the-counter market, "aspirin substitute" usually refers to acetaminophen (Tylenol), which is discussed below as a pain reliever; acetaminophen is not an aspirin substitute for arthritis.

There is a huge market for drugs of this type. Nearly every drug company has tried to invent one and has promoted heavily whatever has been developed. Some of these drugs have been promoted in the financial pages of the newspaper or announced in press releases before the scientific evidence was complete. Clearly, you have to be careful about what you read under such circumstances. But there is some substance to the claims. Many of these drugs are good ones. They may be better for those truly unable to tolerate aspirin. Unfortunately, they are more expensive, newer, and their long-term side effects are less well known. While present evidence suggests that they are slightly safer than aspirin because of fewer stomach problems, they probably should not yet be accepted as less hazardous. Aspirin has been used for centuries and experience with these new drugs is sufficiently short that some side effects may not yet have been discovered.

In perspective, the development of these drugs represents a substantial advance. In part, this is because of the difficult problems posed by the corticosteroids (discussed in the next section). The use of the term *nonsteroidal* to distinguish these compounds underscores the importance of this feature.

In average potency, full doses of these drugs are roughly equivalent to full-dose aspirin. Gastrointestinal side effects, such as heartburn and nausea, are usually less frequent than with aspirin — hence an advantage for those with intolerant stomachs. Available evidence indicates that different drugs can be best for different individuals. These drugs come from several different chemical families and are not interchangeable. You may have to try several to find the best. The major medications in this category are discussed below in alphabetical order, according to brand name. The generic name is given in parentheses.

ADVIL (IBUPROFEN)

See Motrin and Over-the-Counter Ibuprofen.

Advil
200mg

Color: brown

BUTAZOLIDINE (PHENYLBUTAZONE), TANDEARIL (OXYPHENBUTAZONE)

Butazolidine
100mg

Color: orange

Purpose

To reduce inflammation.

Indications

For reduction of inflammation when inflammation is causing harm, as in rheumatoid arthritis.

Dosage

Three or four 100 mg capsules spread throughout the day. Short courses of treatment given for gout or local conditions may be six capsules the first day, then five, four, three, two, and one on successive days for a six-day course.

Side Effects

Unfortunately, phenylbutazone and oxyphenbutazone can be hazardous. These were the first anti-inflammatory agents to be developed and we have had some 20 years of experience with them. We now know that on rare occasions they can cause serious problems with the blood, essentially killing all of the white cells or red cells. These conditions, termed *aplastic anemia* or *agranulocytosis*, can be fatal. They are very rare, occurring in perhaps one person in every 10,000. When encountered, the conditions are sometimes reversible after the drug is stopped, and they don't seem to occur if the drug is used only for a short period. Because of this toxicity, most doctors use the other drugs described below in preference to Butazolidine. This may be unfortunate, since Butazolidine is a very effective medication in many instances.

Irritation of the stomach lining may also occur, with nausea, heartburn, indigestion, and occasionally vomiting. Some persons retain fluid with Butazolidine and a low-salt diet is recommended. Allergic reactions, including rash, are rare.

Special Hints

For nausea, spread the dose out a little through the day and take the capsules on a full stomach, perhaps half an hour after meals. If you don't have a meal at that time, take an antacid half an hour before the medication. Occasionally, some people will have better luck with Tandearil if stomach upset with Butazolidine is a major problem. Watch your weight; if it goes up you are probably retaining fluid. If so, reduce the salt in your diet (see Chapter 13), and be alert for any signs of shortness of breath. If shortness of breath occurs, call the doctor without delay.

While you are taking this drug, blood counts are recommended by most doctors, even though these tests do not protect you against the bad reaction. Possibly, however, they may enable an adverse reaction to be discovered more quickly. Blood counts every two weeks for the first three months and once a month thereafter are recommended by many doctors. For a short six-day course, no blood tests are required by most doctors. You should be able to tell if this is going to be a good drug for you within one week. If you haven't noticed major benefit, you may want to discuss a change in medication with your doctor.

CLINORIL (SULINDAC)

Clinoril (Sulindac)
150mg and 200mg

Color: bright yellow

Purpose

To reduce inflammation, to reduce pain slightly.

Indications

For anti-inflammatory action and mild pain relief.

Dosage

One 150 mg tablet twice a day. This drug also comes in a 200 mg tablet and dosage may be increased to 200 mg twice a day if needed. Maximum recommended dose is 400 mg a day.

Side Effects

Gastrointestinal side effects, with irritation of the stomach lining, are the most common, and include nausea, indigestion, and heartburn. Stomach pain has been reported in 10 percent of subjects, and nausea, diarrhea, constipation, headache, and rash in from 3 to 9 percent. Ringing in the ears, fluid retention, itching, and nervousness have been reported. A few persons have had bleeding from the stomach. Allergic reactions are rare. The use of aspirin in combination with this drug is not recommended by the manufacturer, since aspirin apparently decreases absorption from the intestine.

Special Hints

Sulindac has no particular advantages or disadvantages compared with the other anti-inflammatory agents described in this section. At this writing, Clinoril is one of the most expensive of these agents. It has been promoted beyond its worth as a "miracle" agent; new drugs are not necessarily improvements.

For stomach upset, take the pills after meals; skip a dose or two if necessary. Antacids may be used for gastrointestinal problems and may sometimes help. Check with your doctor if the distress continues. Maximum therapeutic effect is achieved after about six weeks of treatment, but you should be able to see a major effect in the first week if Clinoril is going to be a really good drug for you.

DOLOBID (DIFLUNISAL)

Dolobid
250mg

Color: pink

Dolobid
500mg

Color: white

Purpose

To reduce inflammation and slightly reduce pain

Indications

For anti-inflammatory action and mild pain relief

Dosage

For osteoarthritis, 500 to 700 mg daily is equal to six to ten 300 mg regular aspirin. For rheumatoid arthritis 1000 mg daily has been shown to be as effective as twelve to fourteen 300 mg (regular) aspirin.

Side Effects

This drug is generally well tolerated. Three to 9 percent of people taking this drug may have some stomach pain or diarrhea.

Special Hints

Dolobid is one of the newest of the nonsteroidal drugs and more studies are needed to determine its usefulness when compared to other nonsteroidal anti-inflammatory drugs. At this time, it does not seem to have any particular advantages or disadvantages.

FELDENE (PIROXICAM)

Feldene
20mg

Color: dark red

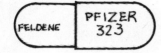

Purpose

To reduce inflammation; to reduce pain slightly.

Indications

For anti-inflammatory activity and mild pain in rheumatoid arthritis, local conditions, and sometimes cartilage degeneration (osteoarthritis).

Dosage

One 20 mg tablet once daily. Do not exceed this dosage. This is a long-acting drug, and it need be taken only once daily.

Side Effects

The drug has been generally well tolerated, although gastrointestinal symptoms including irritation of the stomach lining do still occur, as well as nausea, indigestion, and heartburn. Allergic reactions, including skin rashes or asthma, are very rare. Peptic ulceration can occur, particularly if the recommended dosage is exceeded. Fluid retention is only very occasionally a problem.

Special Hints

Since this is a long-acting drug, some seven to twelve days are required before the benefits are apparent, and full benefits may not be clear until six weeks or more. Aspirin should be avoided in general. Dosage recommendations and indications for use in children have not been established. Some patients with rheumatoid arthritis or osteoarthritis prefer Feldene, particularly because of its relatively mild gastrointestinal toxicity and because of the convenience of once-a-day dosage. On the other hand, there has been no long-term experience with the drug, and it is felt to be a symptomatic medication rather than one that might alter the underlying disease.

INDOCIN (INDOMETHACIN)

Indocin
25mg and 50mg

Color: blue/white

Purpose

To reduce inflammation, to slightly reduce pain.

Indications

For reduction of inflammation and for mild pain relief.

Dosage

One 25 mg capsule three to four times daily. For men or large women, doses totaling as high as 150 to 200 mg (six to eight capsules) may be required and tolerated each day. It is also available in 50 mg capsules and in a 75-mg sustained release form which needs to be taken only twice daily.

Side Effects

Irritation of the stomach lining, including nausea, indigestion, and heartburn, occurs with a number of people. Allergic reactions (including skin rash or asthma) are very rare. The biggest problem is headache and a bit of a goofy feeling reported by some patients. This problem often goes away after two or three weeks.

Special Hints

Many doctors find Indocin to be rather weak for treatment of rheumatoid arthritis in early stages, although it is sometimes effective in later stages. In a long-term illness, maximum effect may take six weeks or so, but you should be able to tell within one week if it is going to be a major help. This is the cheapest of the new nonsteroidal drugs, so if it works you may save money.

There are some problems with absorption of Indocin from the intestine. If you take it after meals, you have less stomach irritation, but some people do not absorb the drug very well. So for maximum effect you need to take it on an empty stomach and for maximum comfort to take it on a full stomach. Trial and error may be necessary to establish the best regimen for you. Aspirin poses another problem. When some individuals take aspirin with Indocin, the Indocin is not absorbed from the intestine. Usually you will not want to take these two drugs together, since you will get more irritation of the stomach lining but no more therapeutic effect than if you just took the aspirin. If this drug makes you feel mentally or emotionally fuzzy for more than the first few weeks, we think that is a good reason to discuss a change in medication with your doctor.

MECLOMEN (MECLOFENAMATE)

Meclomen (Meclofenamate sodium)
100mg

Color: orange/off white

Purpose

To reduce inflammation; to reduce pain slightly.

Indications

For anti-inflammatory action in attachment arthritis, synovitis, local conditions, and occasionally with degenerative cartilage changes.

Dosage

The total daily dosage is 200 to 400 mg, usually administered in three or four equal doses. The drug is supplied in 50 mg and 100 mg capsules.

Side Effects

Gastrointestinal side effects are most commonly reported and include diarrhea in approximately one-quarter of patients, nausea in 11 percent, and other gastrointestinal problems in 10 percent. Over the long term, at least one-third of patients will have at least one episode of diarrhea. The diarrhea is sufficiently severe to require discontinuation of treatment in approximately 4 percent of patients. A variety of other generally minor side effects have been reported but do not appear to be at all common.

Special Hints

This drug was introduced in 1980, and has been used relatively little. It is probably comparable in effectiveness to the other nonsteroidal agents. It is not yet recommended for children, and its effects have not been studied in patients with very severe rheumatoid arthritis. It may be taken with meals or milk to control gastrointestinal complaints.

Maximum effect is achieved after about six weeks of treatment, but you should be able to see a major effect in the first week if it is going to be a really good drug for you. Avoidance of aspirin and other medications while taking this drug is advisable but not essential.

MOTRIN AND RUFEN (IBUPROFEN) ADVIL AND NUPRIN (OVER-THE-COUNTER IBUPROFEN)

Motrin

Color: 600 mg — yellow
       400mg — red-orange

Motrin and Rufen are the same drug, ibuprofen, produced by two different companies.

Purpose

To reduce inflammation, to slightly reduce pain.

Indications

For anti-inflammatory action and mild pain relief.

Dosage

One or two 400 mg tablets three times daily. Maximum daily recommended dosage is 2400 mg, or six tablets.

Side Effects

Gastrointestinal side effects, with irritation of the stomach lining, are the most common, and include nausea, indigestion, and heartburn. Allergic reactions are rare and the drug is generally well tolerated. A very few individuals have been observed who have had *aseptic meningitis* apparently related to this drug. Here, the person experiences headache, fever, and stiff neck, and examination of the spinal fluid shows an increase in the protein and cells. The syndrome resolves when the drug is stopped, but can come back again if the drug is given again. Occasionally, individuals may retain fluid with this medication.

Special Hints

Motrin is not consistently useful for the treatment of rheumatoid arthritis. Overall, many doctors are beginning to feel that it is one of the weaker therapeutic agents in this group. If you are not getting enough relief from it, you may wish to discuss a change in medication with your doctor. Avoidance of aspirin and other medications while taking Motrin is advisable but not essential. It is absorbed reasonably well even on a full stomach, so if you have problems with irritation of the stomach take the drug after an antacid or after a meal. Maximum effect is achieved after about six weeks of treatment, but you should be able to see a major effect in the first week if it is going to be a really good drug for you.

Over-the-Counter Ibuprofen

Recently, the Food and Drug Administration has allowed the sale of ibuprofen without a prescription with a smaller, 200 mg, tablet size. This historic ruling has added a third minor analgesic, ibuprofen, to the two drugs previously available, aspirin and acetaminophen. The decision was made after careful review of many studies indicating that ibuprofen was at least as effective as the previously available drugs, and possibly less toxic, at relieving minor pain. Advil and Nuprin are the trade names for over-the-counter ibuprofen, and they are already heavily advertised and heavily used.

What does this mean for the patient with arthritis? Relatively little. Most arthritis patients need at least 2400 mg of ibuprofen per day, and twelve tablets a day rather than four to six is a bit of a nuisance. And it is hard to save money, since the cost per milligram is set so that it is about the same by prescription or over-the-counter. If you need anti-inflammatory doses of ibuprofen, you should be seeing your doctor every so often anyway, so do not use the availability of the product over-the-counter as an excuse to stay away from the doctor. Also, many health insurance plans will not pay for medication unless it is purchased by prescription. So, our recommendation remains that ibuprofen for arthritis be used on a prescription basis unless just an occasional tablet is required for pain.

NALFON (FENOPROFEN)

Nalfon

Color: 300mg — dark yellow/yellow
      600mg — orange-yellow

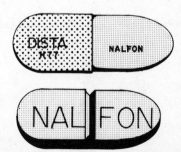

Purpose

To reduce inflammation, to slightly reduce pain.

Indications

For anti-inflammatory activity and mild pain relief in rheumatoid arthritis, local conditions, and sometimes cartilage degeneration (osteoarthritis).

Dosage

One or two 300 mg capsules three or four times a day. Maximum recommended dosage is ten tablets daily. It is now available in 600 mg capsules, with a maximum dosage of five tablets daily.

Side Effects

Irritation of the stomach lining is the most frequent side effect and includes nausea, indigestion, and heartburn. Allergic reactions including skin rash or asthma are very rare. Fluid retention is only very occasionally a problem.

Special Hints

For stomach irritation, reduce the dose, spread it out more throughout the day, or take the drug after meals or after antacid. Maximum effect may take six weeks or more, but you should see major benefit in the first week if the drug is going to be a great help to you. Aspirin should be avoided in general, although the evidence for its effect on the absorption of Nalfon is controversial. Nalfon is quite useful in rheumatoid arthritis and is preferred by many individuals to aspirin on the basis of better effect on the disease as well as less bothersome side effects. It has found uses in osteoarthritis, particularly of the hip.

NAPROSYN (NAPROXEN)

Naprosyn
250mg
375mg
500mg

Color: light yellow

Purpose

To reduce inflammation, to slightly reduce pain.

Indications

For anti-inflammatory action and mild pain relief.

Dosage

One tablet two or three times a day. Maximum recommended dosage is 1000 mg a day.

Side Effects

Gastrointestinal side effects, with irritation of the stomach lining, are the most common and include nausea, indigestion, and heartburn. Skin rash and other allergic problems are very rare. Fluid retention has been reported in a few individuals.

Special Hints

Naprosyn has an advantage over some drugs in this class by having a longer "half-life." Thus, you do not have to take as many tablets as with the other medicines in this group. Each tablet lasts from 8 to 12 hours. In general, aspirin should be avoided, since it interferes with Naprosyn in some individuals. If you notice fluid retention, reduce your salt intake (see Chapter 13), and discuss a change in medication with your doctor. Naprosyn is liked by many people because of the small number of tablets required. It is quite effective in rheumatoid arthritis and is preferred by some people over aspirin and other drugs of this group. Degenerative arthritis of the hip also responds. If you have stomach irritation, try taking the tablets on a full stomach or after antacids. Although absorption may be slightly decreased, you may be more comfortable overall.

NUPRIN (IBUPROFEN)

See Motrin and Over-the-Counter Ibuprofen.

Nuprin
200mg

Color: yellow

RUFEN (IBUPROFEN)

See Motrin.

Rufen
400mg

Color: bright pink

TOLECTIN (TOLMETIN SODIUM)

Tolectin
200mg

Color: white

Purpose

To reduce inflammation, to reduce pain slightly.

Indications

For anti-inflammatory action and mild pain relief.

Dosage

Two 200 mg tablets three or four times daily. Maximum recommended dosage is 2000 mg, or ten tablets daily. Larger tablet sizes may soon be available.

Side Effects

The most frequent side effects are gastrointestinal, as with other drugs of this group. Irritation of the stomach lining can cause nausea, heartburn, and indigestion. Occasionally, individuals note fluid retention. Allergic reactions such as rash or asthma are very rare.

Special Hints

For irritation of the stomach, decrease the dose or spread the tablets out throughout the day. Absorption will be slightly decreased if you take the drug after meals or after antacids, but greater comfort may result. Aspirin and other drugs of this class may potentially interfere with absorption and the best rule is to take just one drug at a time. Tolectin is useful in rheumatoid arthritis. It has found use in degenerative arthritis of the hip and for treatment of local conditions. As with other drugs of this group, certain individuals will prefer Tolectin to all other drugs of the group.

NEWLY RELEASED NONSTEROIDAL MEDICATIONS

A number of new, nonsteroidal anti-inflammatory drugs (NSAIDs), relatively similar to those just discussed, are in the process of review by the Food and Drug Administration of the United States. Many of these drugs are currently being used in foreign countries and appear to have a role in the treatment of osteoarthritis and rheumatoid arthritis. The review process by our Food and Drug Administration now takes approximately four to five years, and it is not possible to predict whether or not a new agent will be released or after what period. Given our current knowledge, none of these new drugs will be dramatically different from drugs that are already available, so not too much is being lost by these delays. Also, a new drug is less well understood in terms of toxicity and benefits than a drug for which there has been wide use in our own country.

On the other hand, our experience has been that individual patients often do better with one or another nonsteroidal drug; therefore, a wide choice of drugs is helpful for finding the drug that causes you the least toxicity and the drug that gives you the most benefit.

Most of these new drugs are propionic acids, similar to the ibuprofen, naproxen, and fenoprofen described in detail above. The newer propionic acid agents include ketoprofen (Orudis), fenbufen, carprofen, pirprofen, oxaprozin, and some others. Several acetic acids similar to indomethacin and sulindac are also under development, including fenclofenac, diclofenac, and others. Proquazone, a nonacetic, nonsteroidal anti-inflammatory agent, belongs to a different class of drugs than any agents currently available and hence might have new properties. This drug is expected to be called Arthrex.

Some of these drugs have been formulated to have less gastrointestinal toxicity than their predecessor, and they may actually be safer agents. Often, on the other hand, the agents that cause the fewest side effects turn out to be the least powerful drugs for the management of arthritis.

In general, when considering one of the new agents, rely on your doctor's advice. If you have been having a lot of trouble with stomach upset from drugs, then it might be a good idea to try one of the agents that causes less gastrointestinal difficulty. If you have not been getting the desired effect from the drugs of one chemical class, sometimes it is useful to try the drugs of a different class. It is possible that some new drugs will be better for rheumatoid arthritis and others better for osteoarthritis or other forms of arthritis. But treat each of these drugs with respect and consider that it is always possible for a drug, particularly a new drug, to be responsible for a new symptom problem that develops while you are taking the medication.

CORTICOSTEROIDS (PREDNISONE)

In about 1950, a widely heralded miracle occurred — the introduction of cortisone for the treatment of arthritis. The Nobel prize was awarded to the doctors who developed this drug. Persons with rheumatoid arthritis and other forms of synovitis suddenly noted that the swelling and pain in their joints decreased and that the overall toxicity of the disease disappeared. They felt fine.

The initial enthusiasm for cortisone in arthritis was tremendous. But over the following years, a number of major cautions began to be voiced. Slowly, the cumulative side effects of the cortisonelike drugs began to be recognized. For many individuals, the side effects were clearly greater than any benefits obtained. Cortisone became the model of a drug that provides early benefits but late penalties. Now, with a quarter of a century of experience with these drugs, our perspective is more complete. They represent a major treatment for arthritis, but their use is appropriate in only a relatively small number of cases and then only with full attention to potential complications.

Steroids are natural hormones manufactured by the adrenal glands. When used medically, they are given in doses somewhat higher than the amounts the body generally makes. In these doses they suppress the function of your own adrenal glands and lead to a kind of drug dependency as the gland slowly shrinks. After many months of steroid use, the drug must be withdrawn slowly to allow your own adrenal gland to return to full function, otherwise an "adrenal crisis" can occur in which you just don't have enough hormone. Steroids must be taken exactly as directed and a physician's close advice is always required.

Steroids used in arthritis are all like prednisone in type and are very different from the sex steroids, or androgens taken by athletes, which have no role in treatment of arthritis, and, indeed, probably shouldn't be used by athletes either.

Let's discuss the side effects. They can be divided into categories depending upon the length of time you have been taking the steroid and the dose prescribed. Side effects result from a combination of how high the dose is and how long you have been taking it. If you have been taking steroids for less than one week, side effects are quite rare even if the dose has been high.

If you have been taking high doses for one week to one month, you are at risk for development of ulcers, mental changes including psychosis or depression, infection with bacterial germs, or acne over the skin. The side effects of steroid treatment become most apparent after one month to one year of medium to high dosage. The individual becomes fat in the central parts of the body, with a buffalo hump on the lower neck and wasting of the muscles in the arms and legs. Hair growth increases over the face, skin bruises appear, and stretch marks develop over the abdomen. After years of steroid treatment (even with low doses) there is loss of calcium, resulting in fragile bones. Fractures can occur with only slight injury, particularly in the spine. Cataracts slowly develop and the skin becomes thin and translucent. Some physicians believe that hardening of the arteries occurs more rapidly and that there may be complications of inflammation of the arteries.

Many of these side effects will occur in everyone who takes sufficient doses of cortisone or its relatives for a sufficient period of time. The art of managing arthritis with corticosteroids involves knowing how to minimize these side effects. The physician will work with you to keep the dose as low as possible at all times. If possible, you may be instructed to take the drug only once daily rather than several times daily, since there are fewer side effects when it is taken this way. If you are able to tolerate the drug only every other day, this is even better, for the side effects are then quite minimal. Unfortunately, many people find that the dosage schedules that cause the fewest side effects also give them the least relief.

Steroids are always to be used with great respect and caution. Some experienced doctors still use low-dose corticosteroid treatment in rheumatoid arthritis, demonstrating that the proper indications for use of these drugs is somewhat controversial. High-dose cortisone treatment for uncomplicated rheumatoid arthritis has long been considered bad practice in the United States; it remains the essence of some quack treatments of arthritis, such as those available in Mexican border towns. Corticosteroids are harmful in infectious arthritis and should not be given by mouth in local conditions or in osteoarthritis.

There are three ways to give corticosteroids. They can be taken by mouth, they can be given by injection into the painful area, or an injection of adrenal cortical stimulating hormone (ACTH) can be given to cause an individual's own adrenal gland to increase production of hormones. Prednisone (or prednisolone) is the steroid usually given by mouth and is the reference steroid discussed here. There are perhaps 20 different steroid drugs now available. Cortisone itself retains too much fluid and the second drug developed, hydrocortisone, has the same deficit. The fluorinated steroids, such as triamcinolone, cause greater problems with muscle wasting than does prednisone. The steroids sold by brand name are about 20 times as expensive as prednisone and do not have any major advantages. Hence, there is little reason to use any of these other compounds for administration of steroids by mouth. Use prednisone.

PREDNISONE

Prednisone
5mg

Color: white

Purpose

To reduce inflammation, to suppress immunological responses.

Indications

For suppression of serious systemic manifestations of connective tissue disease, such as kidney involvement. Occasionally, for use in suppressing the inflammation of rheumatoid arthritis.

Dosage

The normal body makes the equivalent of about 5 to 7.5 mg of prednisone each day. "Low-dose" prednisone treatment is from 5 to 10 mg. A "moderate dose" ranges from 15 to 30 mg per day and a "high dose" from 40 to 60 mg per day, or even higher. The drug is often most effective when given in several doses throughout the day, but side effects are least when the same total daily dose is given as infrequently as possible.

Side Effects

Prednisone causes all of the side effects of the corticosteroids listed above. Allergy is extremely rare. Side effects are related to dose and to duration of treatment. The side effects are major and include fatal complications. Psychological dependency often occurs and complicates efforts to get off the drug once you have begun.

Special Hints

Discuss the need for prednisone very carefully with your doctor before beginning. The decision to start steroid treatment for a chronic disease is a major one and you want to be sure that the drug is essential. You may want a second opinion if the explanation does not completely satisfy you. When you take prednisone, follow your doctor's instructions very closely. With some drugs it does not make much difference if you start and stop them on your own, but prednisone must be taken extremely regularly and exactly as prescribed. You will want to help your doctor decrease your dose of prednisone whenever possible, even if this does cause some increase in your symptoms.

A funny thing happens when you reduce the dose of prednisone; a syndrome called *steroid fibrositis* can cause increased stiffness and pain for a week or ten days after each dose reduction. Sometimes this is interpreted as return of the arthritis and the opportunity to reduce the dose of prednisone is lost. If you are going to take prednisone for a long time, ask your doctor about taking some vitamin D along with it. There is some evidence, still controversial, that the loss of bone, the most critical long-term side effect, can be reduced if you take vitamin D.

If you are having some side effects, ask your doctor about once-a-day or every-other-day use of the prednisone. Watch your salt intake and keep it low, since there is a tendency to retain fluid with prednisone. Watch your diet as well, since you will be fighting an increase in appetite and a tendency to put on unseemly fat. If you stay active and limit the calories you take in, you can minimize many of the ugly side effects of the steroid medication and can improve the strength of the bones and the muscles. If you are taking a corticosteroid other than prednisone by mouth, ask your physician if it is all right to switch to the equivalent dose of prednisone. (See Chapter 13 for further hints on nutrition.)

STEROID INJECTIONS (DEPO-MEDROL, MANY OTHERS)

Purpose

To reduce inflammation in a local area.

Indications

Noninfectious inflammation and pain in a particular region of the body. Or a widespread arthritis with one or two areas causing most of the problem.

Dosage

Dosage varies depending upon the preparation and purpose desired. The frequency of injection is more important. Usually injections should not be repeated more frequently than every six weeks and a limit of three injections in a single area is observed by many physicians.

Side Effects

Steroid injections resemble a very short course of prednisone by mouth and therefore have few side effects. They result in a high concentration of the steroid in the area that is inflamed and can have quite a pronounced effect in reducing this inflammation. If a single area is injected many times, the injection appears to cause damage in that area. This has resulted in serious problems in frequently injected areas, such as the elbows of baseball pitchers. Some studies suggest that as few as ten injections can cause increased bone destruction; hence most doctors stop injecting well before this time.

Special Hints

If one area of your body is giving you a lot of trouble, an injection frequently makes sense. The response to the first injection will tell you quite accurately how much sense it makes. If you get excellent relief that lasts for many months, reinjection is indicated if the problem returns. The steroid injections contain a "long-acting" steroid, but it is in the body for only a few days. The effects may last much longer than this, however, since a cycle of inflammation and injury may be broken by the injection. If you get relief for only a few days, then injection is not going to be a very useful treatment for you. If you get no relief at all or an increase in pain, this is an obvious sign that other kinds of treatment should be sought. If you can find a "trigger point" on your body where pressure reproduces your major pain, then injection of this trigger point is frequently beneficial. Occasionally, persons with osteoarthritis get benefit from injections, but injections are usually not helpful unless there is inflammation in the area.

GOLD SALTS AND PENICILLAMINE

These are major-league drugs, although no one knows exactly why they are so effective in so many individuals. They provide dramatic benefits to over two-thirds of persons with severe rheumatoid arthritis. Each has major side effects that require stopping treatment for at least one-quarter of the users and that may in rare cases be fatal. Gold salts and penicillamine are two very different kinds of drugs, but there are striking similarities in the type and magnitude of good effects and in the type of side effects. Neither appears to be of use in any category other than rheumatoid arthritis, but the scientific proof of their effectiveness in RA is impressive.

These agents can result in remission of the arthritis. In perhaps one-quarter of users the disease will actually be so well controlled that neither doctor nor patient can find any evidence of it. Usually these drugs have to be continued in order to maintain the remission, but the effects can be more dramatic than with any other agent to reduce inflammation, except possibly some of the more dangerous immunosuppressant drugs. Individuals who use these drugs must accept certain significant hazards, but there is a good chance of very major benefit. In rheumatoid arthritis, these drugs have been proven to retard the process of joint destruction.

If you are not able to tolerate one of these drugs, you may be able to tolerate the other. If you don't get a good response from one, you may from the other. After failure with one drug, the chances decrease a little, but success with the second drug is still common.

Which should be used first? No one knows. In England, penicillamine is usually used first. In the United States, it is gold. Gold requires a visit to the doctor every week for a while. With costs of blood tests, the total dollar cost of the initial course of injectable gold may be $800 or more.

Penicillamine can be taken by mouth, and while the drug itself is expensive, the total cost may be less. In terms of effectiveness and in risk, you can consider these two drugs about the same.

MYOCHRISINE, SOLGANOL (GOLD SALTS)
Purpose

To reduce inflammation and retard disease progression.

Indications

Rheumatoid arthritis that is not responsive to less hazardous medications or is severe and rapidly progressive.

Dosage

50 mg per week by intramuscular injection for 20 weeks, then one to two injections per month thereafter. Many doctors use smaller doses for the first two injections to test for allergic reactions to the injections. Sometimes doctors will give more or less than this standard dosage depending upon your body size and response to treatment. "Maintenance" gold treatment refers to injections after the first 20 weeks (which result in about 100 mg of total gold). The dosage and duration of maintenance therapy varies quite a bit; with good responses, the gold maintenance may be continued for many years, with injections given every two to six weeks. Maintenance dosage may be much lower — from 10 to 25 mg. The duration is more important than the dosage.

Side Effects

The gold salts accumulate very slowly in the tissues of the joints and in other parts of the body. Hence, side effects usually occur only after a considerable amount of gold has been received, although allergic reactions can occur even with the initial injection. The major side effects have to do with the skin, the kidneys, and the blood cells. The skin may develop a rash, usually occurring after ten or more injections, with big red spots or blotches, often itchy. If the rash remains a minor problem, the drug may be cautiously continued, but occasionally a very serious rash occurs following gold injections.

The kidney can be damaged so that protein leaks out of the body through the urine. This is called *nephrosis* or the *nephrotic syndrome* if it is severe. When it is recognized and the drug is stopped, the nephrosis usually goes away, but cases have been reported in which it did not reverse. The blood cell problems are the most dangerous. They can affect either the white blood cells or the platelets, those blood cells that control the clotting of the blood. In each case, the gold causes the bone marrow to stop making the particular blood cell. If the white cells are not made, the body becomes susceptible to serious infections that can be fatal. If the platelets are not made, the body is subject to serious bleeding episodes that can be fatal. These problems almost always reverse when the drug is stopped, but reversal may take a number of weeks, during which time the person is at risk for a major medical problem.

There are other side effects, such as ulcers in the mouth, a mild toxic effect on the liver, or nausea, but they usually are not as troublesome. Overall, about one-quarter of users have to stop their course of treatment because of the side effects. One or two percent of users experience a significant side effect; the other users don't really notice very much of a problem, even though a serious side effect may be about to occur. Less than one in a thousand times there may be a fatal side effect. With careful monitoring, the drug is reasonably safe and its benefits justify its use, since over 70 percent of those treated with gold show moderate or marked improvement. However, you must maintain your respect for this treatment and keep up regular blood tests to detect early side effects. One final note: Most side effects occur during the first initial period of 20 injections. Serious side effects during the maintenance period are unusual.

Special Hints

You must learn to be patient with gold treatment. The gold accumulates slowly in the body and responses are almost never seen in the first 10 weeks of treatment. Improvement begins slowly after that and major improvement is usually evident by the end of 1000 mg, or 20 weeks. Similarly, if the drug is stopped, it requires many months before the effect is totally lost. In one famous study, the gold group was still doing better than the control group two years after the drug had been stopped, although most of the effect of the drug had been lost by that time. After a side effect, many doctors will suggest that the drug be tried again. Often, this can be worthwhile if the approach is very cautious, since the drug is frequently tolerated the second time around. At the Arthritis Center we do not try gold salts again if there has been a problem with the blood, but we will use it again cautiously after mild skin reactions or mild amounts of protein loss through the urine.

To minimize the chance of serious side effects, most doctors recommend that a check be made of the urine for protein leakage, of the white cells and the platelets, and that the patient is questioned about skin rash before every injection. This is good practice. Unfortunately, the combination of 20 doctor visits, 20 injections, 20 urinalyses, 20 blood counts, and so forth, makes the cost of initiating gold treatment approximately $800 when pursued in this manner. There are some ways to decrease this cost while preserving the safety. You can ask your doctor to prescribe some test kits so that you can test your urine for protein at home. This is a very easy technique. You can ask if it is possible to have just a platelet smear and a white count rather than a complete blood count each time. You can inquire whether it is possible to have the nurse give an injection after checking the blood count without actually having a doctor visit every week. And, some people have successfully been given their own shots at home with the help of their family, although this is not acceptable to many. By using such techniques, you can save half to three-quarters of the cost of a course of gold treatment.

RIDAURA (AURANOFIN)

Ridaura
3mg

Color: brown and white

Purpose

To reduce inflammation in rheumatoid arthritis and retard disease progression. (This drug is "oral gold.")

Indications

For anti-inflammatory activity in rheumatoid arthritis.

Dosage

Average dosage is 6 mg daily. The drug is slowly absorbed and distributed through the body, and weeks to months may be required before full therapeutic effect is achieved. This drug appears closely similar to intramuscular gold injections in effectiveness, and the mechanism of action is probably the same. Side effects are much reduced compared to those of intramuscular gold injections.

Side Effects

The most common side effect is dose-related diarrhea, which occurs at some time in approximately one-third of treated patients but requires discontinuation in only about 2 percent of patients. Skin rash has occurred in 4 percent, mild kidney problems in 1 percent, and problems with the platelets in half of 1 percent of patients.

Special Hints

This drug is useful in rheumatoid arthritis, for which it may be a very important drug. It is not believed to be effective in osteoarthritis, gout, or minor rheumatic conditions. It may or may not have an eventual role in psoriatic arthritis, ankylosing spondylitis, and the arthritis of children. If diarrhea is encountered, the dose should be reduced. As with intramuscular gold injections, patients should be monitored periodically for blood complications, skin rash, and protein loss in the urine. Follow your doctor's advice for the particular tests required and the frequencies with which they are needed. This is a powerful drug and needs to be used with respect.

PENICILLAMINE (CUPRIMINE)

Penicillamine (Cuprimine)

Color: 125mg — gray/yellow
250mg — yellow

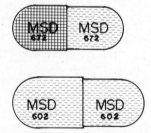

Purpose

To reduce inflammation and retard disease progression.

Indications

Rheumatoid arthritis that is not responsive to less hazardous medications or is severe and rapidly progressive.

Dosage

Usually 250 mg (one tablet or two 125 mg tablets) per day for one month, then two tablets (500 mg) a day for one month, then three tablets (750 mg) per day for one month, and finally four tablets (1000 mg) per day. Dosage is usually not increased rapidly, and may be increased even more slowly than this. After remission, the drug can be continued indefinitely, usually at a reduced dosage. And if a good result is obtained earlier, you can stop with the lower dose.

Side Effects

These closely parallel those noted above for gold injections. The major side effects are skin rash, protein leakage through the urine, or a decrease in production of the blood cells. Additionally, individuals may have nausea, and some notice a metallic taste in their mouth or a decreased sense of taste. Penicillamine weakens the connective tissue so that the healing of a cut is delayed, and a scar may not have the same strength it would have without the penicillamine. So, stitches following a cut should be left in for a longer period of time, and wound healing should be expected to be delayed. Surgery under these circumstances may be more difficult.

Special Hints

Penicillamine takes a number of months to reach its full therapeutic effect and the effect persists for a long time after you stop taking the drug. Responses usually take from three to six months but can be as late as nine months after the drug is begun. Because of the risk of side effects, doctors have now adopted the "go low, go slow" approach given in the dosage schedule above. When full doses were begun earlier, the frequency of side effects was higher. Even now, only about three-quarters of individuals will complete the treatment and the remainder will have some side effects, approximately the same as those listed for gold salts. The drug may be tried again after a side effect if the side effect has been mild. We do not try the drug again if there has been a problem with the blood counts, but may cautiously try it if there has been a minor problem with protein in the urine, a minor skin rash, or minor nausea.

Monitoring for side effects has to be carefully performed. Usually a blood count or smear, a urinalysis for protein leakage, and questioning of the person about side effects are required every two weeks or even more frequently. It should be noted that with both penicillamine and gold, careful monitoring improves your chances of not having a serious side effect, but does not eliminate them. These drugs contain an intrinsic hazard that no physician can eliminate. Again, you can negotiate to have some of the drug monitoring done by a local laboratory and review the results yourself, check your own urine for protein, and so forth, if you desire. Most doctors who use these drugs a good deal have evolved some method of minimizing the cost of the monitoring. Again, after the first six months, side effects are relatively rare but still do occur. Some individuals will have an excellent response to the penicillamine, even though they never get up to the full dosage of 1000 mg per day.

PLAQUENIL (HYDROXYCHLOROQUINE)

Plaquenil
200mg

Color: white

Purpose

To reduce inflammation and possibly to retard disease progression in rheumatoid arthritis.

Indications

Rheumatoid arthritis that is active.

Dosage

One to two tablets (200 to 400 mg) per day.

Side Effects

This is the best tolerated of all drugs used for rheumatoid arthritis, and side effects are unusual. With a very few people, gastric upset or muscular weakness may result. Consideration needs to be given to the possibility of eye toxicity, which is an occasional complication of antimalarial drugs. This is a rare complication and appears to be always reversible if the possibility is regularly monitored by periodic eye examinations after the first year of treatment.

Special Hints

Plaquenil takes six weeks to begin to show an effect, and full effect can take up to 12 weeks, so plan on at least a 12-month trial. The eye complications appear to be much less common with Plaquenil than with chloroquine, the antimalarial drug that used to be used most often. They seldom if ever are seen with less than one year of treatment at recommended dosage. Bright sunlight seems to increase the frequency of eye damage, so we recommend using sunglasses and wide-brimmed hats for sun protection. We recommend eye examinations after one year of continuous treatment and at three-month intervals thereafter. This should give ample warning of any problems. Do not exceed two tablets daily. Since the drug is so well tolerated, both tablets may be taken together in the morning. The good effects of this drug are long-lasting, and continue for weeks or months after the drug is stopped. Overall, this is the safest drug available for treatment of rheumatoid arthritis; it should be used with respect but not fear.

AZULFIDINE (SULPHASALAZINE)

Azulfidine
500mg

Color: yellow

Azulfidine EN-tabs
500mg

Color: yellow

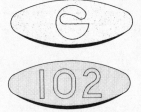

Purpose

To reduce inflammation and possibly to retard disease progression in rheumatoid arthritis.

Indications

Rheumatoid arthritis that is active.

Dosage

Three or four 500 mg tablets daily, taken spread out as two or three doses over the day. Dosage may be increased to as many as six 500 mg tablets, usually taken as two tablets three times daily.

Side Effects

This is a sulfa drug, and should not be taken by people with an allergy to sulfa. Allergy is unusual, and may take the form of rash, wheezing, itching, fever, or jaundice. Azulfidine may cause gastric distress or other side effects in some patients. Blood tests should be done every so often to detect any (rare) effects on the blood cells or platelets. Most people, probably four out of five, experience no trouble whatsoever.

Special Hints

Azulfidine is used in patients with inflammatory problems with the bowels, where it reduces the inflammation, at least in part because of an antibiotic effect on the bacteria that live in the bowel. Recently, British scientists have found that it has a major effect on rheumatoid arthritis and this has been confirmed by investigators in the United States. No one knows how it works, but it is very effective in some patients. It takes a month or more before the effects begin to be noticed, and full effects may take three or more months. Usually if you are not going to tolerate the drug, you will know in a week or so.

IMMUNOSUPPRESSANT DRUGS

These immunosuppressant drugs are experimental and powerful. They are prescribed in certain cases of rheumatoid arthritis because they can reduce the number of inflammatory cells present around the joint. However, these drugs are seldom required for effective treatment.

The immune response helps the body recognize and fight foreign particles and viruses. When it goes wrong, it can cause allergy or autoimmune disease. In this case, antibodies from the immune system attack the body's own tissues, causing disease. Immunosuppressant drugs can tone down this reaction.

Some of these drugs work by *cytotoxic* action. They kill rapidly dividing cells much like an X-ray beam. Since in some diseases the most rapidly dividing cells are the bad ones, the overall effect of the drugs is good. Others of these drugs antagonize the chemical system inside the cell, such as the purine system or the folate system. From the patient's standpoint, it doesn't make too much difference how they work and they can all be considered about the same. Keep in mind that they are powerful and dangerous.

The major short-term worry with these drugs is that they can destroy bone-marrow cells. The bone-marrow cells make red cells that carry oxygen, white cells that fight infection, and platelets that stop bleeding. Any of these blood-cell types can be suppressed by taking enough of these drugs and even if there seem to be enough white cells, dangerous infections can occur.

These infections are often called "opportunistic"; different kinds of germs cause them than those that cause infections in healthy people. For example, patients are often afflicted with Herpes Zoster (shingles) and can be prone to infections from types of fungus that is around all the time but seldom cause disease. Or, a rare bacterial infection can occur. These infections can be difficult to treat and sometimes hard to diagnose.

For patients who have taken immunosuppressant drugs for several years, there is some concern about cancer. Although it seems to be extremely rare in humans, these drugs *do* cause cancer in some laboratory animals. It seems that if humans are afflicted, it is only after years of treatment. Methotrexate, unlike the true cytotoxic drugs, does not seem to cause cancer.

After considering all these dangers, we really don't know how to compare them to other drugs. Although there is some danger of cancer, the alternative might be prednisone with all of its potential problems. It is possible that these drugs are actually less dangerous than some of the drugs with which we are currently comfortable.

The diseases for which these drugs may be most useful are as follows in descending order: In Wegener's granulomatosis, previously fatal, these drugs are usually curative. They seem helpful in severe polyarteritis. They are probably useful in resistant severe dermatomyositis or polymyositis. They are probably helpful in severe kidney disease or systemic lupus. They are helpful in psoriatic arthritis and rheumatoid arthritis, but here they should be reserved for the most seriously affected patients.

METHOTREXATE

Methotrexate
2.5mg

Color: yellow

Purpose

For immunosuppression.

Indications

Steroid-resistant dermatomyositis or polymyositis, severe psoriatic arthritis, severe rheumatoid arthritis.

Dosage

Often this drug is given intravenously or intramuscularly at intervals of one week to ten days followed by a week during which no drug is taken. The dose ranges from 20 to 40 mg each injection. If taken orally, the dose is usually 5 to 15 mg per week given in 2 or 3 doses, 8 to 12 hours apart.

Side Effects

These include opportunistic infections, mouth ulcers, stomach problems, and the possibility of late development of cancer. Damage to the liver, a special side effect of this drug, is particularly a problem if the drug is taken orally every day. When taken orally, this drug is absorbed by the intestine and passes through the liver on the way to general circulation. If taken every day, cirrhosis and severe problems with the liver can occur. As a result, most doctors have discontinued this method of administration. Instead the drug is given intermittently, so that the liver has an opportunity to heal. Problems can still occur with the newer dose schedules, but are much less frequent.

Special Hints

This drug is remarkably effective in many cases of rheumatoid arthritis and has become the preferred drug (over cyclophosphamide and azathioprine) for many patients. Regular blood tests are required as with all of these drugs. Some doctors recommend liver biopsy to be sure that the liver is normal before starting the drug. However, this procedure is dangerous and seems unnecessary as long as blood liver tests are normal before the drug is started. The blood liver tests should be checked every so often, perhaps at three- or six-week intervals during treatment, and the drug should be stopped if there is any suspicion of difficulty. Since alcohol can damage the liver, alcohol intake should be extremely moderate during this period of methotrexate treatment.

CYTOXAN (CYCLOPHOSPHAMIDE)

Cytoxan

Color: 25mg — white
      50mg — white with blue flecks

Purpose

For immunosuppression.

Indications

Wegener's granulomatosis, severe systemic lupus erythematosus, poly-arteritis, possibly severe rheumatoid arthritis.

Dosage

Usual dose is 100 to 150 mg (two to three tablets) daily.

Side Effects

The dosage can be adjusted so that the white count is maintained in the low normal range. Severe bone-marrow cell depression can occur and cancer has followed use in laboratory animals. Opportunistic infections can result. Special side effects of Cytoxan include hair loss, which can be quite extensive, but usually reverses after the drug is discontinued, and bladder irritation. The drug is eliminated from the body through the kidneys and the eliminated products can cause blisters on the inside of the bladder. Scarring of the bladder and possibly even cancer of the bladder can occur after long-term use. Additionally, there is a decrease in the sperm count and, in women of child-bearing age, there is damage to the eggs which can cause sterility. These effects are reversible at first, but irreversible later. Stomach or intestinal upset is noted by some patients.

Special Hints

Cytoxan may be the strongest of the immunosuppressant agents and it is probably the most toxic. Nitrogen mustard, which must be given by vein, is a similar drug with many of the same side effects. It is not used frequently. The bladder side effects can be minimized by drinking large amounts of water, and all patients taking this drug should try to drink an extra two quarts of liquid each day beyond their usual intake. This dilutes the toxic products in the bladder and minimizes the damage. Don't take this drug at bedtime because the urine concentrates over-night and stays in your bladder too long. Use of this drug should be reconsidered by patients planning to have children. Regular blood counts, every one or two weeks to start and no less frequently than once a month later, are required.

LEUKERAN (CHLORAMBUCIL)

Leukeran
2mg

Color: white

Purpose

For immunosuppression.

Indications

Wegener's granulomatosis, severe systemic lupus erythematosus, poly-arteritis, possibly severe rheumatoid arthritis.

Dosage

One to six 2 mg tablets daily.

Side Effects

The same as Cytoxan (cyclophosphamide), except hair loss is less fre-quent and the bladder side effects do not occur.

Special Hints

For reasons that are unclear, chlorambucil is not used as frequently as cyclophosphamide, although some doctors prefer it. The bone-marrow suppression is less predictable and can happen a bit more suddenly with chlorambucil according to some investigators. With any of these drugs, regular blood counts, every one to two weeks to begin with and no less frequently than once a month later, are required.

IMURAN (AZATHIOPRINE), 6-MP (6-MERCAPTOPURINE)

Imuran
50mg

Color: yellow

Purpose

For immunosuppression.

Indications

Severe systemic lupus erythematosus, severe rheumatoid arthritis, severe psoriatic arthritis, steroid-resistant polymyositis or dermatomyositis.

Dosage

100 to 150 mg (two or three tablets) daily is the usual dose.

Side Effects

Azathioprine and 6-mercaptopurine are closely related drugs with almost identical actions. Azathioprine is the most frequently used. Side effects include opportunistic infections and possibility of late development of cancer. Gastrointestinal (stomach) distress is occasionally noted. Hair loss is unusual and there appears to be little effect on the sperm or the eggs. There are no bladder problems. Although liver damage has been reported, the drug is usually well tolerated.

Special Hints

Regular blood tests are required. Patients taking these drugs should never take allopurinol (Zyloprim), since the combination of drugs can be fatal. Once the patient responds to this drug, it is often possible to reduce the dose. Theoretically, this decreases the risk of late side effects. Azathioprine has been shown to slow down the progression of rheumatoid arthritis and is very effective in some patients. Most people seem not to have any side effects but there is still concern about what might happen over the long run.

DRUGS TO REDUCE PAIN

This section is included mainly to emphasize that pain-reducing drugs have little place in the treatment of arthritis. Consider their four major disadvantages. First, they don't do anything for the arthritis, they just cover it up. Second, they help defeat the pain mechanism that tells you when you are doing something that is injuring your body. If you suppress it, you may injure your body without being aware of it. Third, the body adjusts to pain medicines, so that they aren't very effective over the long term. This phenomenon is called *tolerance* and develops to some extent with all of the drugs we commonly use. Fourth, pain medicines can have major side effects. The side effects range from stomach distress to constipation to mental changes. Most of these drugs are "downers," which you don't need if you have arthritis. You need to be able to cope with a somewhat more difficult living situation than the average person. These drugs decrease your ability to solve problems.

Many individuals develop a tragic dependence on these agents. In arthritis, the addiction is somewhat different from what we usually imagine. Most persons with arthritis are not truly addicted to codeine or Percodan or Demerol. They are psychologically dependent on these drugs as a crutch and become inordinately concerned with an attempt to eliminate every last symptom. These agents conflict with the attempt to achieve independent living.

By and large, use these drugs only for the short term and only when resting the sore part, so that you don't reinjure it while the pain is suppressed. Drugs mentioned first in this list are less harmful than those listed later. Drugs to reduce inflammation, discussed above, may reduce pain through direct pain action as well as through reduction of inflammation. This is preferable.

These same principles hold for a number of less common pain relievers not described in the following section.

ACETAMINOPHEN (TYLENOL, OTHER BRANDS)

Tylenol
325mg

Color: white

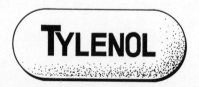

Extra-Strength Tylenol
500mg

Color: tablet or caplet — white

Purpose

For temporary relief of minor pain.

Indications

Mild temporary pain, particularly with cartilage degeneration (osteoarthritis).

Dosage

Two tablets (ten grains) every four hours as needed.

Side Effects

Minimal. Unlike aspirin, acetaminophen usually does not upset the stomach, does not cause ringing in the ears, does not affect the clotting of the blood, does not interact with other medications, and is about as safe as can be. Of course, as with any drug, there are occasional problems, but this drug is frequently recommended in place of aspirin for children because of its greater safety. And acetaminophen is the only drug in this category that is not addictive.

Special Hints

Acetaminophen is not anti-inflammatory; thus it is not an aspirin substitute in the treatment of arthritis. If the condition is not an inflammatory one, then it may be approximately as useful as aspirin with fewer side effects. It is only a mild pain reliever and therefore has fewer disadvantages than the following agents. It is relatively inexpensive. Advertised names, such as Tylenol, may be more expensive than other acetaminophens.

DARVON (DARVON COMPOUND, DARVO-TRAN, DARVOCET, DARVOCET-N, PROPOXYPHENE)

Darvon
32mg and 65mg

Color: pink

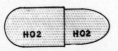 

Purpose

Mild pain relief.

Indications

For short-term use in decreasing mild pain.

Dosage

One-half grain (32 mg) or one grain (65 mg) every four hours as needed for pain.

Side Effects

These drugs are widely promoted and widely used with a reasonably good safety record. In some cases, side effects may be due to the aspirin or other medication in combination with the Darvon. Most worrisome to us has been the mentally dull feeling that many individuals report, often described as a gray semiunhappy fog. Others do not seem to notice this effect. Side reactions include dizziness, headache, sedation, somnolence, paradoxical excitement, skin rash, and gastrointestinal disturbances.

Special Hints

Darvon is not anti-inflammatory and is thus not an aspirin substitute. The pain relief given is approximately equal to aspirin in most cases. The drug is more expensive than aspirin or acetaminophen. It can induce dependence, particularly after long-term use.

CODEINE (EMPIRIN #1, 2, 3, 4; ASPIRIN WITH CODEINE #1, 2, 3, 4)

Codeine (Empirin)
No. 1 grl/8   No. 2 grl/4
No. 3 grl/2   No. 4 grl

Color: white

Purpose

Moderate pain relief.

Indications

For moderate pain relief over the short term.

Dosage

For some curious reason, the strengths of codeine are often coded in numbers. For example, Empirin with codeine #1 or just Empirin #1 contains one-eighth grain or 8 mg of codeine per tablet, #2 contains one-fourth grain or 16 mg, #3 contains one-half grain or 32 mg, and #4 contains one grain or 65 mg of codeine phosphate. A common dosage is a #3 tablet —32 mg codeine) every four hours as needed for pain.

Side Effects

The side effects are proportional to the dosage. The more you take, the more side effects you are likely to have. Allergic reactions are quite rare.

Codeine is a narcotic. Thus, it can lead to addiction, with tolerance and drug dependence. Frequently in persons with arthritis it leads to constipation and sometimes a set of complications including fecal impaction and diverticuli. More worrisome is the way that persons using codeine seem to lose their will to cope. The person taking codeine for many years sometimes seems sluggish and generally depressed. We don't really know if the codeine is responsible, but we do think that codeine often makes it more difficult for the person with arthritis to cope with the very real problems that abound.

PERCODAN (PERCOBARB, PERCOGESIC)

Percodan

Color: 0060-0122
    light yellow
    0060-0123 (Percodan-Demi)
    pink

Purpose

For pain relief.

Indications

For short-term relief of moderate to severe pain.

Dosage

One tablet every six hours as needed.

Side Effects

Percodan is a curious combination drug. The basic narcotic is oxycodone, to which is added aspirin and other minor pain relievers. Combination drugs have a number of theoretical disadvantages, but Percodan is a strong and effective reliever of pain. It does require a special prescription because it is a strong narcotic and the hazards of serious addiction are present. The manufacturers state that the habit-forming potentialities are somewhat less than morphine and somewhat greater than codeine. The drug is usually well tolerated.

Special Hints

Percodan is a good drug for people with cancer, but it is very dangerous in the treatment of arthritis. It is not an anti-inflammatory agent and does not work directly on any of the disease processes. It is habit forming and it does break the pain reflex. It is a mental depressant and serious addiction can result.

DEMEROL (MEPERIDINE)

Demerol

Color: pink/dark pink splotches

Purpose

For relief of severe pain.

Indications

For temporary relief of severe pain, as with a bad fracture that has been immobilized.

Dosage

Various preparations come with 25 mg, 50 mg, or 100 mg of Demerol. One tablet every four hours for pain is a typical dose. Dose is increased for more severe pain and decreased for milder pain.

Side Effects

Demerol is a major narcotic approximately equivalent to morphine in pain relief and in addiction potential. Tolerance develops and increasing doses may be required. Drug dependence and severe withdrawal symptoms may be seen if the drug is stopped. Psychological dependence also occurs. The underlying disease may be covered up and serious symptoms may be masked. Nausea, vomiting, constipation, and a variety of other side effects may occur.

Special Hints

This is not a drug for the treatment of arthritis. Stay away from it.

TRANQUILIZERS

Valium, Librium, and other drugs of this ilk are among the most-prescribed drugs in this country. They do not help arthritis, they act to depress the patient, and they should be avoided by persons with arthritis whenever possible.

AN EXTRA WORD ABOUT ASPIRIN AND MONEY

It is well known that aspirin is the best single drug for arthritis. However, there are many types of aspirin at many different prices and in combination with many different drugs. By knowing how to buy and reading labels, you can spend much less on your arthritis medications. In fact, the difference between the least expensive and the most expensive aspirin is nearly $67 per year.

When buying, there are a few things to remember:

1. All you need is aspirin. The addition of such drugs as caffeine, which you find in Anacin, will do nothing for your arthritis.

2. Buffered aspirin or coated aspirin are always more expensive. Before buying, try all the hints for taking regular aspirin.

3. Tylenol or other drugs with acetaminophen *are not* the same as aspirin. They have *no effect* on the inflammation of joints.

The following prices were obtained at a well-known chain drugstore in early 1986. While prices will change, the relative prices should remain about the same.

ASPIRIN AND ASPIRIN PRODUCTS

Drug Name	Number of Pills per Bottle	Content Each Pill	Price per 100	Price per Pill	Price of Equivalent of 8 5-gr Aspirin per Day for 1 Year
Anacin	100	Aspirin, 400 mg or 5.7 gr + 30 mg caffeine	$3.70	$.04	$ 96.20
Arthritis Pain Formula	100	Aspirin, 7.5 gr + an antacid	7.19	.07	143.80
Anacin, Maximum Strength	100	Aspirin, 500 mg or 7.5 gr + 32 mg caffeine	4.60	.05	87.40
Bayer Aspirin	100	Aspirin, 5 gr or 325 mg	2.33	.02	67.57
Maximum Bayer	60	Aspirin, 10 gr	4.65	.05	69.75
Generic Buffered Aspirin	100	Aspirin, 5 gr or 324 mg + an antacid	1.49	.01	43.21
Encaprin	200	Aspirin, 7.5 gr	4.65	.05	88.35
Ecotrin, Maximum Strength	150	Aspirin, 7.7 gr or 300 mg	7.77	.07	147.63
Long's Easy-to-Swallow Aspirin	100	Aspirin, 5 gr	1.19	.01	34.51
Norwich Aspirin	500	Aspirin, 5 gr	0.40	.004	11.60

OVER-THE-COUNTER NONSTEROIDAL DRUGS

Drug Name	Number of Pills per Bottle	Content Each Pill	Price per 100	Price per Pill	Price of Equivalent of 8 5-gr Aspirin per Day for 1 Year
Nuprin	100	200 mg Ibuprofen	7.19	.07	208.51
Advil	165	200 mg Ibuprofen	5.45	.04	158.05

15

Working With Your Doctor
A Joint Venture

CHOOSING A DOCTOR

There are many different kinds of doctors and sometimes it is difficult to know what kind to work with for what. Fortunately, most people with arthritis do not need a specialist on a regular basis. Therefore, it often is best to find a doctor who can help you with all of your health problems. For most of you, this will be an internist or a family practitioner.

An *internist* is a doctor who has had special training in the care of adults. Internists take care of all common adult health problems, including arthritis. A *family practitioner* has special training in taking care of all the common health problems that occur in a family. Thus a family practitioner may assist at the birth of a baby and also take care of grandmother's arthritis. As a general rule, the fewer doctors you have, the better coordinated your health care will be.

For people with difficult arthritis, a specialist might be the answer. If your arthritis is resistant to treatment or if you have severe rheumatoid arthritis, the expertise of a *rheumatologist* might be of value.

Rheumatologists are internists with additional training in arthritis and rheumatic diseases. To find a rheumatologist, look in the yellow pages of your telephone book or ask your doctor if he or she thinks that a referral might be of help. (Unfortunately, not all communities have physicians listed by specialty.) You can also get a list of rheumatologists in your area from the nearest office of the Arthritis Foundation. Finally, you can call your County Medical Society for a list of their members who are rheumatologists. An orthopedic surgeon also can be of great help in particular instances, and do not hesitate to ask your doctor to arrange a consultation. Remember that not all doctors belong to the Medical Society.

A word of warning: Some people spend a great deal of time and money doctor shopping. They go from doctor to doctor looking for a cure. Unfortunately, doctor shoppers get cheated from having one physician really get to know them and thus be able to build an optimal treatment plan over time. The best advice is to find a doctor you like and stick with him or her. Sometimes, with severe arthritis, nearly all of your care should be provided by a rheumatologist.

COMMUNICATING WITH YOUR DOCTOR

This is a huge area and probably causes more concern than anyone wishes to admit. Let us first examine expectations.

When someone goes to the doctor he or she usually wants relief of symptoms and/or reassurance that all is well. He or she may also want information about health or illness. On the other hand, the doctor wants the person to get well and usually feels that the best way to accomplish this is for him or her to follow medical advice. The patient often recognizes the need for communication more than the doctor does.

A shortened version of a typical encounter with a doctor might go something like this:

PATIENT: Doctor, I have a pain in my knee.

DOCTOR: How long have you had the pain? (Meanwhile, the knee is being examined.)

PATIENT: Six months.

DOCTOR: I think you have arthritis. I want you to exercise, take aspirin, and lose some weight. Let me know how you are feeling in a month or so.

Meanwhile, the patient is thinking: "How much aspirin? Does he want me to jog at my age? What does weight have to do with all this?

Is this just what he tells everyone? Why doesn't he give me some good medicine? He just wants to get rid of me."

And the doctor is thinking: "I know he or she won't do those things; my patients never do. I wish I knew how to get people to realize that aspirin, proper exercise, and weight control are the best treatment for osteoarthritis. Patients always want a miracle cure and we just don't have one."

The fact is that arthritis can be a very frustrating disease for both doctor and patient, because there often is not any quick, easy answer.

Before continuing, let's look at some research answers about doctors and patients. Doctors think that patients ought to know a great deal about arthritis. They also believe that patients know very little. The reality is that patients know more than doctors think they know, but patients often don't ask questions or seek information. And, some of the information patients have is wrong.

Thus, there are several important things you can do to communicate with your doctor:

1. Ask questions. To be sure you don't forget, go to your appointment with a written list of questions. Don't wait for the doctor to ask for questions. Ask them when you first enter the office. Research has shown that it is important to ask questions early in the appointment. Later, if you don't understand something, ask. "How many aspirin?" "What kind of exercise?" "Why should I lose weight?" "What do you mean by *synovitis*?"

2. If for some reason you know you won't or can't follow the doctor's advice, let the doctor know. For example, "I won't take aspirin. It gives me stomach problems." "Clinoril may be good but I can't afford it." "I hate exercise." "I would like to lose weight but I can't seem to give up chocolate and need help."

   Often, if your doctor knows why you can't or won't follow advice, alternate suggestions can be made to help you over the hump. If you don't share your problems there is no help of finding solutions.

3. If you have problems with your treatment let your doctor know. Don't just stop or change doctors. Since much arthritis treatment is trial and error you must work with your doctor.

4. Finally, don't be afraid to ask financial questions. You have a right to know how much an appointment will cost. You can ask the receptionist when you call the doctor's office. If you feel a treatment is too expensive, ask if there are any alternatives. For example, an

exercise class at the YMCA or senior citizen center may be as effective as working with a physical therapist. You may be able to test your own urine at home. There are almost always solutions to such problems if they are discussed.

In short, to get the most from your doctor, be a CAD:

Come prepared, Ask questions, Discuss problems

PROBLEMS

Over the years, we have heard many complaints about doctors and would like to discuss a few of these.

1. **My doctor never has time.**   It is true that physicians are busy. Unlike people in business, they do not have a product to sell. All they have is time. If you know you want to talk with your doctor, ask for more time when you make your appointment. Most offices are run so that a certain amount of time is allotted for each type of visit. For example, 5 to 10 minutes for a brief follow-up, 15 to 20 minutes for a short visit, and 30 to 45 minutes for a complete physical. You can ask for as much time as you need. However, you must indicate the amount of time you want when you make your appointment, not when you arrive at the office. Also, you should expect to pay for this extra time.

Another way you can make time is to go to the office prepared. Bring a written list of your questions. Give this list to the doctor when you first start the visit and be sure they are answered before you leave. Don't count on remembering. All of us are a little nervous when we visit the doctor, and it's very easy to forget.

2. **All my doctor does is try one pill after another.** Unfortunately, there is no way your physician can know for sure what medication will work for you. You may need to try a number of medications before you find the right combination. This trial-and-error method can be expensive. Therefore, when you start a new medication, ask for a prescription for only a week or two, with refills of the prescription permitted. In this way, you can try the medication, and if it doesn't work, you will not have a lot of expensive pills to throw away. Sometimes the doctor will have free sample packages available. Don't be discouraged if you have to try several different medications. Also, don't hesitate to let your doctor know if you have problems with a medication or if it is not working. If you have a problem with a drug and do not have an appointment in the near future, contact your doctor by phone.

3. **My doctor never tells me anything about my medications.** Again, time is often a factor, or maybe you didn't ask. If you want more information about your medications, first ask your physician. If this is not satisfactory, you can ask the pharmacist that fills the prescription. Pharmacists provide an underutilized resource for drug information.

4. **There is no cure; there is nothing my doctor can do anyway.** Yes and no. While it is true there is no cure for many types of arthritis, there is a great deal that can be done. Diabetes is another disease with no cure. However, insulin and appropriate medical care enable diabetics to live nearly normal lives. No diabetic would think of saying that because there was no cure, physicians can't do anything. For people with arthritis, medical attention can do a number of things. First, just knowing what one has relieves a lot of worry; this in itself is valuable. Second, physicians may be able to suggest treatment to make life easier. Third, with many types of arthritis, medical treatment can control the disease or keep it from progressing. Thus, while it is true that doctors often can't cure arthritis, they often can help you help yourself in living more comfortably.

5. **My doctor uses language I can't understand.** Unfortunately, doctors are so used to talking "doctor-talk" that they sometimes exclude the rest of us. They don't do this on purpose or even realize they are doing it. The situation is simple. If you don't understand something, ask. Never be afraid to speak up.

6. **My doctor ignores my ideas about self-care.** Now, this is a hard one. Often, doctors are not trained in use of alternative therapies, and like all of us, tend to downplay those things they don't know about. On the other hand, physicians have a responsibility to let you know when a proposed treatment has little scientific merit or is just plain harmful. At our Arthritis Center, we get hundreds of calls a year about all kinds of treatments. We tell people what we know or don't know and try to warn them of possible harms. We, and your doctor, also feel a responsibility to prevent folks from spending large amounts of money on treatments with potential harm or no effect.

If your doctor disregards your ideas, then you have an extra responsibility to find out about the treatment. Generally, if the treatment is free or inexpensive and does not have harmful side effects, go ahead and try it if you wish. On the other hand, be very conscious of expensive treatments (someone is making money off of you). Treatments that promise a cure, or anything with the word *miracle* attached to it, are *never* miracle cures!!

7. **My doctor never listens to me.**   A good relationship takes two people, people who have similar ideas and are able to communicate. If you feel your doctor is not listening to you, we suggest that you discuss this with him or her. You can start by saying something like, "Dr. Jones, sometimes I feel you don't hear what I'm saying." This takes some nerve, but we can promise that it will open up the communication process.

Another way to get your doctor to listen is to be brief and to the point. You might even practice before going in. Think out exactly what you want to say; this will make it easier.

8. **I don't feel comfortable talking with my doctor.**   This is a problem common to many of us. We have already discussed many ways you can make communication easier. Here is one more. Whenever you want to have a serious conversation with your doctor, wear your own clothes. It is hard to feel confident in your underwear or while wearing an examination gown.

Sometimes the personalities of the physician and the patient just don't fit. If you have tried to open up communications and it hasn't worked, then maybe it is time to find a new doctor. Not every patient can like every doctor and vice versa. Doctors sometimes wish they had the option of changing patients. You do have this option, and when necessary, don't be afraid to use it. Good patient-physician relationships are important.

A doctor's addendum: I never have seen a person with arthritis that I couldn't help. There are some individuals, however, that I have not helped. In every such case, the communication broke down. Sometimes I am short of time or short of temper. Sometimes the person doesn't listen or doesn't hear or doesn't understand. Often, a preconceived opinion is the problem. "Aspirin won't work." "My neighbor couldn't tolerate that drug." "I hardly eat a thing." "She seems too old to exercise." "I don't think he would understand." Or a person who reports being worse never filled a prescription, stopped an exercise program after two days, decreased medication ("It was too expensive"), and never mentioned the problem. A solid half of the blame lies with the doctor. Sometimes we do not listen or have our own preconceived ideas. No matter how hard we try we don't always get it right. But the other half of the blame lies with the patient. Tell it true and straight and we can help. This is a partnership. We don't always have to agree to get good results. But the give-and-take of direct communication is essential.

A NOTE ABOUT SURGERY

Surgery is one of the things that you might want to talk over with your doctor. The greatest single advances in treatment of rheumatoid arthritis and osteoarthritis over the past twenty years have been surgical, the development of joint replacement surgery. We do not discuss surgery for arthritis in detail in this book, since every decision is individual and requires a great deal of discussion between you and your doctor. When considering surgery: Think it over. Talk it over. Decide. Here are some general considerations, however, to keep in mind if the question of surgery comes up.

1. Arthritis surgery is seldom urgent. These are "elective" operations, and should be undertaken when the disability and pain from a joint have failed medical management and justify the pain, risk, and expense of the operation. You don't have to decide in a hurry. Think it over. Get multiple opinions. Take your time.

2. Arthritis surgery does not replace medical management and self-management. Instead, it means that you must pay particular care to the other parts of your treatment program.

3. Surgery is most likely to be productive when you are in good shape. Your exercise program is critical to getting you ready for surgery and for recovering from it.

4. Surgery works best when one joint (or a few joints) are causing most of your problems. If many, many joints are severely affected, surgery on just a few will have limited benefit.

5. Surgery works better on large joints than on small ones. The intricacies of operation and recovery are such that the post-operative scarring in small joints may reduce the benefit.

6. Total joint replacement usually provides better results than lesser operations. The most dramatic surgical advances have been made in replacement operations for the joints. In particular, pain relief is greatest with the operations.

7. Total joint replacement is most predictably beneficial in the hip, then in the knee. Procedures for other joints are newer, less established, but getting better.

8. Total joint replacements don't last forever. A good average for hip replacement, for example, is fifteen years. Procedures for replacement of the replacement are good and getting better, and the new

models of prosthetic joints look like they will last longer than the older ones.

9. Hand operations, with or without artificial joints, are better at restoring appearance than at restoring function. Best results tend to be when a deformity, such as a sublaxation, is itself interfering with function.

10. Relatively simple operations, such as bunionectomy or removal of a Morton's neuroma, can sometimes be dramatically effective.

The Arthritis Foundation

The "AF" is a truly marvelous institution. It sponsors programs in public education and professional education, supports young professionals establishing research careers in arthritis, and provides direct support for research activities. The AF leads the fight for increased government programs of research and service.

The Arthritis Foundation consists of a national office and local chapters around the country. You will usually want to contact the local chapter, which can advise you of doctors and clinics in your area, provide instructional materials, and occasionally may be able to help with financial problems. There may be a schedule of activities you might wish to attend. Or you might want to volunteer your efforts in support of the chapter.

National Office
The Arthritis Foundation
1314 Spring St., N.W.
Atlanta, Georgia 30309
Telephone: (404) 872-7100

ARTHRITIS FOUNDATION CHAPTERS

ALABAMA

Alabama Chapter
13 Office Park Circle, Rm. 14
Birmingham, Alabama 35223
Tel: (205) 870-4700

South Alabama Chapter
304 Little Flower Avenue
Mobile, Alabama 36606
Tel: (205) 471-1725

ARIZONA

Central Arizona Chapter
2102 W. Indian School Rd.,
Suite 9
Phoenix, Arizona 85015
Tel: (602) 264-7679

Southern Arizona Chapter
4520 E. Grant Road
Tucson, Arizona 85712
Tel: (602) 326-2811

ARKANSAS

Arkansas Chapter
6213 Lee Avenue
Little Rock, Arkansas 72205
Tel: (501) 664-7242

CALIFORNIA

Northeastern California Division
1722 "J" St., Suite 321
Sacramento, California 95814
Tel: (916) 446-7246

Northern California Chapter
203 Willow St., Suite 201
San Francisco, California 94109
Tel: (415) 673-6882

San Diego Area Chapter
6154 Mission Gorge Rd.,
Suite 110
San Diego, California 92120
Tel: (619) 280-0304

Southern California Chapter
4311 Wilshire Boulevard
Los Angeles, California 90010
Tel: (213) 938-6111

COLORADO

Rocky Mountain Chapter
234 Columbine St., Suite 210
P.O. Box 6919
Denver, Colorado 80206
Tel: (303) 399-5065

CONNECTICUT

Connecticut Chapter
370 Silas Deane Highway
Wethersfield, Connecticut 06109
Tel: (203) 563-1177

DELAWARE

Delaware Chapter
234 Philadelphia Pike, Suite 1
Wilmington, Delaware 19809
Tel: (302) 764-8254

DISTRICT OF COLUMBIA

Metropolitan Washington Chapter
1901 Ft. Myer Drive, Suite 507
Arlington, Virginia 22209
Tel: (703) 276-7555

FLORIDA

Florida Chapter
3205 Manatee Ave. West
Bradenton, Florida 33505
Tel: (813) 748-1300

GEORGIA

Georgia Chapter
1340 Spring Street, NW
Atlanta, Georgia 30309
Tel: (404) 873-3240
Toll Free: 1-800-282-7023

HAWAII

Hawaii Chapter
200 North Vineyard, Suite 503
Honolulu, Hawaii 96817
Tel: (808) 523-7561

IDAHO

Idaho Chapter
700 Robbins Rd., Suite 1
Boise, Idaho 83702
Tel: (208) 344-7102

ILLINOIS

Central Illinois Chapter
Allied Agencies Center
320 East Armstrong Ave.,
Rm. 102
Peoria, Illinois 61603
Tel: (309) 672-6337

Illinois Chapter
79 W. Monroe, Suite 1120
Chicago, Illinois 60603
Tel: (312) 782-1367

INDIANA

Indiana Chapter
1010 East 86th Street
Indianapolis, Indiana 46240
Tel: (317) 844-3341

IOWA

Iowa Chapter
1501 Ingersoll Ave., Suite 101
Des Moines, Iowa 50309
Tel: (515) 243-6259

KANSAS

Kansas Chapter
1602 East Waterman
Wichita, Kansas 67211
Tel: (316) 263-0116

KENTUCKY

Kentucky Chapter
1381 Bardstown Road
Louisville, Kentucky 40204
Tel: (502) 459-6460

LOUISIANA

Louisiana Chapter
4700 Dryades
New Orleans, Louisiana 70115
Tel: (504) 897-1338

MAINE

Maine Chapter
37 Mill Street
Brunswick, Maine 04011
Tel: (207) 729-4453

MARYLAND

Maryland Chapter
12 West 25th Street
Baltimore, Maryland 21218
Tel: (301) 366-0923

MASSACHUSETTS

Massachusetts Chapter
59 Temple Place
Boston, Massachusetts 02111
Tel: (617) 542-6535

MICHIGAN

Michigan Chapter
23400 Michigan Ave., Suite 605
Dearborn, Michigan 48124
Tel: (313) 561-9096

MINNESOTA

Minnesota Chapter
122 West Franklin, Suite 440
Minneapolis, Minnesota 55404
Tel: (612) 874-1201

MISSISSIPPI

Mississippi Chapter
6055 Ridgewood Road
Jackson, Mississippi 39211
Tel: (601) 956-3371

MISSOURI

Eastern Missouri Chapter
7315 Manchester
St. Louis, Missouri 63143
Tel: (314) 644-3488

**Western Missouri
Greater Kansas City Chapter**
8301 State Line, Suite 117
Kansas City, Missouri 64114
Tel: (816) 361-7002

MONTANA

Montana Chapter
P.O. Box 20994
Billings, Montana 59102
Tel: (406) 248-7602

NEBRASKA

Nebraska Chapter
2229 N. 91st Court, #33
Omaha, Nebraska 68134
Tel: (402) 391-8000

NEVADA

Nevada Division
3160 S. Valley View Blvd.,
Suite 107A
Las Vegas, NV 89102
Tel: (702) 367-1626

NEW HAMPSHIRE

New Hampshire Chapter
P.O. Box 369
35 Pleasant Street
Concord, New Hampshire 03301
Tel: (603) 224-9322

NEW JERSEY

New Jersey Chapter
15 Prospect Lane
Colonia, New Jersey 07067
Tel: (201) 388-0744

NEW MEXICO

New Mexico Chapter
5112 Grand Avenue, N.E.
Albuquerque, New Mexico 87108
Tel: (505) 265-1545

NEW YORK

Central New York Chapter
505 E. Fayette Street, 2nd Floor
Syracuse, New York 13202
Tel: (315) 422-8174

Genesee Valley Chapter
973 East Avenue
Rochester, New York 14607
Tel: (716) 271-3540

Long Island Division
501 Walt Whitman Road
Melville, New York 11747
Tel: (516) 427-8272

New York Chapter
115 East 18th Street
New York, New York 10003
Tel: (212) 477-8310

Northeastern New York Chapter
1237 Central Avenue
Albany, New York 12205
Tel: (518) 459-5082

Western New York Chapter
1370 Niagara Falls Boulevard
Tonawanda, New York 14150
Tel: (716) 837-8600

NORTH CAROLINA

North Carolina Chapter
P.O. Box 2505
3115 Guess Road
Durham, North Carolina 27705
Tel: (919) 477-0286

NORTH DAKOTA

Dakota Chapter
1402 North 39th Street
Fargo, North Dakota 58102
Tel: (701) 282-3653

OHIO

Central Ohio Chapter
2501 N. Star Road
Columbus, Ohio 43221
Tel: (614) 488-0777

Northeastern Ohio Chapter
11416 Bellflower Road
Cleveland, Ohio 44106
Tel: (216) 791-1310

Northwestern Ohio Chapter
4447 Talmadge Road
Toledo, Ohio 43623
Tel: (419) 473-3349

Southwestern Ohio Chapter
2400 Reading Road
Cincinnati, Ohio 45202
Tel: (513) 721-1027

OKLAHOMA

Eastern Oklahoma Chapter
2816 East 51st, Suite 120
Tulsa, Oklahoma 74105
Tel: (918) 743-4526

Oklahoma Chapter
3313 Classen Blvd., Suite 101
Oklahoma City, Oklahoma 73118
Tel: (405) 521-0066

OREGON

Oregon Chapter
Barbur Blvd. Plaza
4445 S.W. Barbur Blvd.
Portland, Oregon 97201
Tel: (503) 222-7246

PENNSYLVANIA

Central Pennsylvania Chapter
P.O. Box 668
2019 Chestnut Street
Camp Hill, Pennsylvania 17011
Tel: (717) 763-0900

Eastern Pennsylvania Chapter
311 So. Juniper St., Suite 201
Philadelphia, Pennsylvania
19107
Tel: (215) 735-5272

Western Pennsylvania Chapter
428 Forbes Ave., Suite 2401
Pittsburgh, Pennsylvania 15219
Tel: (412) 566-1645

RHODE ISLAND

Rhode Island Chapter
850 Waterman Avenue
East Providence, Rhode Island
02914
Tel: (401) 434-5792

SOUTH CAROLINA

South Carolina Chapter
1802 Sumter Street
Columbia, South Carolina 29201
Tel: (803) 254-6702

SOUTH DAKOTA

See North Dakota

TENNESSEE

Middle-East Tennessee Division
210 25th Avenue, N, #1202
Nashville, Tennessee 37203
Tel: (615) 329-3431

West Tennessee Chapter
2600 Poplar Ave., Suite 200
Memphis, Tennessee 38112
Tel: (901) 452-4482

TEXAS

North Texas Chapter
6300 Harry Hines Blvd.,
Suite 211
Exchange Park, Treadway Plaza
Dallas, Texas 75235-5207
Tel: (214) 956-7771

Northwest Texas Chapter
3145 McCart Avenue
Fort Worth, Texas 76110
Tel: (817) 926-7733

South Central Texas Chapter
503 South Main Street
San Antonio, Texas 78204
Tel: (512) 224-4857

Texas Gulf Coast Chapter
9111-A Katy Freeway, Suite 210
Houston, Texas 77024
Tel: (713) 468-6572

West Texas Chapter
2317 34th Street
Lubbock, Texas 79411
Tel: (806) 793-3273

UTAH

Utah Chapter
Graystone Plaza #15
1174 E. 2700 South
Salt Lake City, Utah 84106
Tel: (801) 486-4993

VERMONT

Vermont Chapter
Richardson Place, Suite 3F
2 Church Street
Burlington, Vermont 05401
Tel: (802) 864-4988

VIRGINIA

Virginia Chapter
1900 Byrd Ave., Suite 100
P.O. Box 6772
Richmond, Virginia 23230
Tel: (804) 282-5491

WASHINGTON

Western Washington Chapter
726 Broadway, Suite 103
Seattle, Washington 98122
Tel: (206) 324-9940

WEST VIRGINIA

West Virginia Chapter
P.O. Box 8473
440 Fourth Avenue
South Charleston, West Virginia
25303
Tel: (304) 744-3042

WISCONSIN

Wisconsin Chapter
1442 N. Farwell Ave., Suite 508
Milwaukee, Wisconsin 53202
Tel: (414) 276-0490
Toll Free: 1-800-242-9945

WYOMING — See Colorado

Bibliography

GENERAL

Books

Arthritis Foundation. **Understanding Arthritis,** ed. I. Kushner. New York: Scribner's, 1984.

Barnard, Christiaan, and Peter Evans. **Christiaan Barnard's Program for Living with Arthritis.** New York: Fireside Book, Simon & Schuster, 1984.

Benson, Herbert, and Miriam Klipper. **The Relaxation Response.** New York: Avon, 1976.

Davidson, Paul. **Are You Sure It's Arthritis? A Guide to Soft-Tissue Rheumatism.** New York: Macmillan, 1985.

Downing, George. **The Massage Book.** New York: Random House, 1972.

Epstein, Gloria. **Help Yourself to Chronic Pain Relief: The Patient's Point of View.** Seattle, Wash.: Manchester Group, 1981.

Fries, James F., M.D., **Arthritis: A Comprehensive Guide,** rev. ed. Reading, Mass.: Addison-Wesley, 1986.

Lipton, Sampson. **Conquering Pain.** New York: Arco, 1985.

Madders, Jane. **Stress and Relaxation,** ed. Kenneth Hay. New York: Arco, 1979.

Pantell, Robert H., M.D., James F. Fries, M.D., and Donald M. Vickery, M.D. **Taking Care of Your Child,** rev. ed. Reading, Mass.: Addison-Wesley, 1985.

Vickery, Donald M., M.D., and James F. Fries, M.D. **Take Care of Yourself,** rev. ed. Reading, Mass.: Addison-Wesley, 1986.

Ziebell, Beth. **Wellness: An Arthritis Reality.** Dubuque, Ia., Kendall-Hunt, 1981.

Tapes

Relaxation tapes (by Selma Cole) for people with arthritis are available from the Stanford Arthritis Center, HRP Building, Room 6, Stanford, CA 94305.

NUTRITION
General Nutrition

Brody, Jane. **Jane Brody's Nutrition Book.** New York: Bantam Books, 1982.

Corbin, Cheryl. **Nutrition.** New York: Holt, Rinehart, & Winston, 1981.

Vegetarian Eating

Lappé, Frances. **Diet for a Small Planet.** New York: Ballantine, 1982.

Robertson, Laurel, Carol Flinders, and Bronwen Godfrey. **Laurel's Kitchen: A Handbook for Vegetarian Cookery & Nutrition.** New York: Bantam, 1978.

Weight Control

Ferguson, James M. **Learning to Eat: Behavior Modification for Weight Control.** Palo Alto, Calif.: Bull Publishing, 1975.

Nash, Joyce D., and Linda Ormiston. **Taking Charge of Your Weight and Well-Being.** Palo Alto, Calif.: Bull Publishing, 1978.

Waltz, Julie. **Food Habit Management,** ed. Fay Ainsworth and Susan Sommerman. Edmonds, Wash.: Northwest Learning Associates, 1982.

Index

ARTHRITIS: A Comprehensive Guide to Understanding Your Arthritis

Revised Edition

James F. Fries, M.D.

The Companion Volume to THE ARTHRITIS HELPBOOK
The Book that Answers All Your Questions About Arthritis

You can have much more control over your arthritis than you think. In this enormously helpful book, arthritis expert, Dr. James Fries, has created a program that will help you take an active role in understanding and defeating your arthritis. Fully revised to include the most up-to-date medical information, Dr. Fries' 3-step program shows you how to:

- Identify the kind of arthritis you have

- Work with a doctor to choose the best treatment and medication program

- Cope with the daily problems of pain

Thirty easy-to-read decision charts illustrate when to use home treatment and when to consult a doctor. There's also sensitive advice on dealing with emotional and sexual difficulties and a section that answers common questions about employment. With a wealth of information on all aspects of arthritis, no one who has arthritis can afford to be without this book. To order your copy of ARTHRITIS, simply send in the coupon below to:

> Addison-Wesley Publishing Company
> General Books Division
> Retail Sales
> Reading, MA 01867

Please send me _____copy(ies) of ARTHRITIS: A COMPREHENSIVE GUIDE TO UNDERSTANDING YOUR ARTHRITIS @ $9.95 per copy.

My check or money order for full payment is enclosed. (Add state and local sales tax where applicable. Postage paid by Addison-Wesley.) Please allow 4–6 weeks for delivery.

Name _____

Address _____

City _____State _____Zip _____